ROUTLEDGE LIBRARY EDITIONS: AGING

Volume 17

COMMUNICATION PROBLEMS IN ELDERLY PEOPLE

COMMUNICATION PROBLEMS IN ELDERLY PEOPLE

Practical Approaches to Management

ROSEMARY GRAVELL

LONDON AND NEW YORK

First published in 1988 by Croom Helm Ltd

This edition first published in 2024
by Routledge
4 Park Square, Milton Park, Abingdon, Oxon OX14 4RN

and by Routledge
605 Third Avenue, New York, NY 10158

Routledge is an imprint of the Taylor & Francis Group, an informa business

© 1988 Rosemary Gravell

All rights reserved. No part of this book may be reprinted or reproduced or utilised in any form or by any electronic, mechanical, or other means, now known or hereafter invented, including photocopying and recording, or in any information storage or retrieval system, without permission in writing from the publishers.

Trademark notice: Product or corporate names may be trademarks or registered trademarks, and are used only for identification and explanation without intent to infringe.

British Library Cataloguing in Publication Data
A catalogue record for this book is available from the British Library

ISBN: 978-1-032-67433-9 (Set)
ISBN: 978-1-032-68797-1 (Volume 17) (hbk)
ISBN: 978-1-032-68808-4 (Volume 17) (pbk)
ISBN: 978-1-032-68805-3 (Volume 17) (ebk)

DOI: 10.4324/9781032688053

Publisher's Note
The publisher has gone to great lengths to ensure the quality of this reprint but points out that some imperfections in the original copies may be apparent.

Disclaimer
The publisher has made every effort to trace copyright holders and would welcome correspondence from those they have been unable to trace.

Communication Problems in Elderly People

Practical Approaches to Management

ROSEMARY GRAVELL

CROOM HELM
London & Sydney

© 1988 Rosemary Gravell
Croom Helm Ltd, Provident House,
Burrell Row, Beckenham, Kent BR3 1AT
Croom Helm Australia, 44–50 Waterloo Road,
North Ryde, 2113, New South Wales

British Library Cataloguing in Publication Data

Gravell, Rosemary
 Communication problems in elderly people:
 practical approaches to management. —
 (Therapy in practice).
 1. Geriatrics 2. Communicative disorders
 I. Title II. Series
 618.97′6855 RC952.5

ISBN 0–7099–4634–1

Printed and bound in Great Britain by Mackays of Chatham Ltd, Kent

Contents

Acknowledgements		vii
Foreword *Rosemary Lubinski, Ed.D.*		ix
1.	The Aging Process	1
2.	Traditional Approaches to Assessment and Therapy	19
3.	Counselling	40
4.	Communication and Dementia	52
5.	Sensory Changes, Disorders and Management	74
6.	Hospital and Community	95
7.	The Institutional Environment	107
8.	The Multidisciplinary Team	129
9.	Families	145
10.	The State of the Art	157
References		159
Index		171

In memory of
my father, John R. Moon

Acknowledgements

I would like to thank Jenny Sheridan and Sue Stevens for their invaluable advice and support; Marjorie Moon and Lyn Gregory for their secretarial skills; and Chris Griffin for the artwork.

Foreword

Rosemary Lubinski, Ed.D.
Associate Professor
Dept. of Communicative Disorders and Sciences
State University of New York at Buffalo

The profession of speech-language pathology and audiology devotes itself to the enrichment of communicative skills and opportunities for a wide variety of individuals from infancy to old age. The concept that we have a significant service to offer elderly people, in particular, has only been realised in the past ten to fifteen years. Recently, there has been an awakening to the changes that occur with age in speech physiology, cognition, speech and language processes, and auditory functioning. This has led to an increase in research in these areas and to innovative ways of meeting the communication needs of older people in the community and in long-term care settings. Communication disorders specialists in Great Britain, the United States and Canada meet on a common ground when they devote their research and clinical efforts to better understanding the role of communication for elderly people, the changes that occur with aging, specialised diagnostic methods, and efficient and effective service delivery programmes.

Elderly individuals with communication problems present unique challenges. These challenges stem from the characteristics of elderly people themselves, the stereotypes society has created about the aged, and our own reluctance at times to work with the most severely handicapped, the multiply-impaired, those with progressive disorders, those who are dying, and those who may not visibly appreciate our efforts. It is only by understanding the aging process itself and its relationship to communication, that we can better identify the communication needs of this group and plan appropriate intervention.

Furthermore, communication disorders specialists have also begun to realise that 'remediating' the communication problems of elderly patients without working with significant others in the patient's environment may be futile, inefficient, and inappropriate. Clinical research has clearly indicated that the physical and psychosocial environment of the elderly patient impacts on the patient's motivation to communicate and to carry over improved skills to activities of daily living. The burden to improve communication must be *shared* by the elderly person *and* his or her primary communication partners. Older persons need not only adequate cognitive, speech, language and hearing skills but also ample opportunities to communicate with partners of their choice in stimulating activities. Thus, communication disorders specialists cannot end their treatment at the therapy door but must invite significant others including family, other rehabilitation staff, medical personnel, social service, other patients, volunteers and friends to be a part of the communication therapy process.

This book meets a special need in our growing literature on elderly people and their communication needs. First, it is written by a practitioner, a clinician who works with older people. The perspective taken in this text thus reflects her extensive experience with such people, their care givers, and other rehabilitation specialists. Second, the book reflects a team approach to intervention with elderly clients. Effective intervention is defined from a wholistic and realistic viewpoint. Third, the text integrates the existing literature in the area without being overbearing. The information is synthesised in a coherent, practical way, leading the reader to a better understanding of the problems of working with elderly people and hence more effective ways of service delivery. Finally, the text has an international flavour in that it reflects the author's knowledge of the current state of clinical geriatric intervention in both Great Britain and the United States. Few books offer this valuable integration of two knowledge bases.

As you read this book, ask yourself how important communication is to you now at this point in your personal and professional life. Then project yourself into the future when you, too, will be elderly. Can you imagine the changes that will occur, some positive, many negative? What will being able to communicate mean to you then? It is likely that being able to communicate effectively and meaningfully will be an important part of your life. Our communication lives, twenty, thirty or more years from now, are being sown in the philosophy we create today in our society, our institutions, and our teaching programmes. The more attention we can devote today to improving the communication of elderly people will be reaped in our own lives tomorrow.

1

The Aging Process

Aging is the developmental process that extends throughout life, from 'womb to tomb'. Thus, a person aged twenty will have different abilities, skills and experiences from those he will possess when he is fifty years old, and these in turn will differ from those at eighty years old. Aging causes differences, not deficits, for disease and disorder are not inevitable correlates of old age.

Such a difference can be seen in the communication skills that an individual demonstrates at different points in his life. Aging leads to changes in language comprehension, expression and use, in speech and voice. These changes are more pronounced in the later years of life, and therefore there will be particular demands placed upon the speech therapist who works with an elderly population. These demands will extend from assessment, through planning and management, and must be met if therapy is to be effective.

However, having stated that changes occur with age, and that these changes require a specialised approach, it is not necessarily chronological age that determines the need for special treatment. The overuse and overgeneralisation of chronological age as the criterion for being 'elderly' has contributed enormously to the myths of aging and the negative stereotype which attaches to the status of being old. So which elderly people do require this specialised approach?

It is not difficult to find statistics relating to the huge increase in that proportion of the population aged 65 or over. The US Health Affairs, for example, reported an increase from 5.4 per cent of the population being over 65 years old in 1930 to 11.3 per cent in 1980, and went on to predict that by 2030 there will be 18.3 per cent of the population in this age bracket. Such 'were, are and will be' figures are frequently used in attempts to stimulate a response from Health and Social Services planners. Ouslander and Beck (1982) found that over 65-year-olds in the United States, while forming 11 per cent of the population, used 30 per cent of annual health care costs, 30 per cent of acute beds, and 25 per cent of prescription drugs.

However, the value of such statistics is debatable because they are based on this arbitrary cut-off point of chronological age. While this may be necessary in some instances, such as distribution of pensions and benefits, in many cases it has led to enormous overgeneralisation of facts relating to older members of society. Researchers who have looked at such statistics in more depth have demonstrated this. Roos, Shapiro and Roos (1984), for example, looked at the proportion of hospital days used by over 65-year-olds, and found it was indeed high. However, closer study revealed that 42 per cent of this age group had not been admitted, and that a huge 20 per cent of total hospital days were used by a mere 2 per cent of the so-called elderly people. They also stated that it is a myth that over 65s take up more family practitioner time, and suggest that the elderly population are less often referred on for specialist advice.

What is perhaps most significant in the statistics is that it is the 'old old' whose numbers are increasing most rapidly, as the result of improved medical and social care. In the *British Medical Journal* (April 1985) it was suggested that the total over 65 group will alter little in the next 25 years, but that the 65 to 74-year-old group will decrease, and the 75 to 84-year-old group will rise by 7 per cent, with a phenomenal increase of 34 per cent in the over 85-year-olds. Some claim that the term 'elderly' is usually used, in health care, to refer to the over 75-year-olds, but many researchers continue to use the 65-year-old cut-off point.

However, clinicians seem intuitively to recognise that the term 'elderly' is best applied, not as a result of an arbitrary chronological criterion, but to refer to those who might be described as 'physiologically aged'. Thus the alert 75-year-old who requires no more medical or social care than a 'normal' 45-year-old is not seen by most clinicians as being elderly. The 'physiologically aged', meanwhile, may be viewed clinically as those who suffer from one or more of the mental, physical or socioeconomic conditions that are more likely to occur, and to create problems, in older people. As individuals age the risk that they will experience certain illnesses (for example, depression, dementia, cerebrovascular accident) increases, and the associated likelihood that they will suffer from multiple pathologies grows. These age-linked conditions create very particular management problems.

Speech therapists are as much at fault as other professionals in making generalisations about elderly people, and in neglecting properly to consider the needs of the physiologically aged. Assessment materials and techniques are used as they would be with any adult, and rarely is consideration given to the inherent difficulties in generalising about this older group. Therapy is offered to those alert enough to respond to traditional approaches, but there is little attention paid to the needs of those who are unable to respond to this form of intervention. They, and their carers, are frequently left to cope with the communication difficulty.

Any clinician working with an older population needs a baseline upon which to base clinical judgements; that is, a knowledge of the aging process and how it impinges upon their field of expertise. As Rowe (1985) points out 'Just as children are not merely young versions of adults, the elderly are not simply old adults'.

THE AGING PROCESS

A brief outline of physiological, cognitive, psychological and social changes related to the aging process, and which affect communication, will be given. There are numerous texts which offer a fuller description of such changes, but it is hoped that this short discussion will provide a basis from which practical management decisions may be made.

Effective communication is the transmission of a message between sender and receiver. It requires an individual to have functioning sensori-perceptual, language, cognitive and motor skills, although it is not essential that the medium is auditory-verbal; and also to have adequate opportunity and reason to communicate. Figure 1.1 describes the communication chain and it can be seen how changes in such abilities as hearing and memory will indirectly or directly affect the efficient operation of the communication act.

THE AGING PROCESS

Figure 1.1: Communication chain

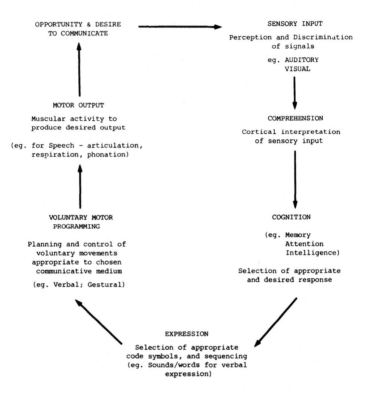

The study of most aspects of the aging process has historically been via cross-sectional design, that is comparing older and younger subjects at one time. This has led to results which are possibly not a function of age *per se*, but of cohort differences. Recognition of this methodological failing led to the introduction of longitudinal studies, which look at one individual at two or more points in time. Again, however, there are flaws, in that results may be due to specific circumstances at the time of testing, and in any case cannot be generalised without reservation to other cohorts. Denney (1981) stresses the need to be aware of such problems in interpreting data relating to the effects of age, and this proviso must apply to some of the research mentioned in the following pages. Indeed Weiss (1971) felt that attempting to study aging was so fraught with difficulties that it 'would make strong men weep'.

Physiological changes

There are age-related changes within most bodily systems, but physiological changes are not related in an .absolute way to chronological aging. In the physiological sense some people age faster or more slowly than others, but in all individuals eventually systems such as the respiratory and cardiovascular will show signs of aging. The respiratory system, which is of course crucial to speech production, is affected by changes in the curvature of the vertebral column, and increased rigidity of the thorax. Reduced pulmonary function results from a decrease in elasticity and power, and anatomical changes in the joints and muscles will further affect functioning. Diseases of the respiratory system (such as bronchitis and pneumonia) are very common in older people.

Sensori-perceptual changes

Sensory changes have been studied in some depth, and it appears that there are both peripheral effects and alterations in central processing. All the special senses — vision, hearing, taste, olfaction and touch — are affected in that there appears to be a lowering of sensitivity. This may be a function of over-cautious responding within a test situation which elevates thresholds.

Visual changes. These include alterations in the cornea, lens and media, and there is a much greater risk of ocular diseases such as cataract and glaucoma. This may impair the older person's ability to utilise non-verbal clues in communication, and specifically to use vision to compensate for decreased auditory acuity. Chapter 5 considers this aspect of aging in greater depth.

Hearing. This has been the focus of much research in the field of gerontology. At the same time, it has frequently been neglected in terms of rehabilitation and management. There appear to be regular alterations in the structures of the inner ear, such as increased stiffness of the basilar membrane, increased viscosity in the tissues of the ear, physical changes in the tectorial membrane and hair cells, and in the endolymph.

These changes may contribute to the condition known as presbyacusis, which is a decrease in hearing acuity particularly marked in the higher frequencies, and which therefore leads to a distorted speech signal input. Other pathologies not uncommon in older populations include tinnitus, noise-induced losses and otosclerosis.

The quality of the auditory signal becomes more crucial to older ears, with less ability to cope with distorted signals. Hearing loss, of whatever aetiology, will often affect the person in the role of the speaker, as well as listener, as the important auditory feed-back loop for monitoring speech will be less efficient. Furthermore, hearing loss — which will be discussed in more detail in Chapter 5 — can have profound effects upon the individual's general behaviour and response to treatment.

Perception may be defined as the way in which the central nervous system makes use of the incoming sensory information. It seems likely that there are alterations in the CNS that limit the capacity to integrate input from several sources, and thus to make processing decisions. Response rigidity and a reduced ability to alter initial perceptions — perhaps as a result of decreased efficiency of sensory feedback mechanisms — will also affect perceptual abilities. Other factors may include problems with concentration and cerebration. A useful summary of sensori-perceptual aging is offered by Corso (1971) among others.

Psychomotor changes

It appears from the literature that reaction time to sensory stimuli is increased, not as a result of muscular changes, but because of changes in central mechanisms (such as diminished arousal levels) and in psychological factors (for example, caution in responding). The stereotyped view of older people with slowed movements and reduced ability is due not to the aging process as such, but to some overgeneralisation of the incidence of physical complaints and disorders. Such conditions as arthritis and rheumatism are far from uncommon in the older population.

Cognitive changes

Various academics have attempted, from the sea of available data, to create models of cognitive development. Among them is Schaie, who in 1977–78 proposed stages of Acquisition, Achievement, Responsibility, Executive functioning and — in old age — of Reintegration. He saw this final stage as more pragmatic and functional, with greater influence exerted by motivational and attitudinal variables, and a subconscious rejection of redundant and irrelevant information. It may thus be that changes in cognitive functioning that occur with age are in fact beneficial, and represent more adaptive ways of coping with alterations in life situation.

Memory. This is not a unitary phenomenon, as can be seen in Figure 1.2, but is a term to represent various types or levels. Smith and Fullerton (1981) reviewed the experimental evidence relating to iconic (visual), echoic (auditory) or haptic (movement) memory (that is, immediate recall, as in auditory digit repetition tasks) and found it to be shortened in older subjects, but that this had little, if any, functional relevance. Short-term memory is the name given to the system (or set of interlinked systems) which allows storage of information on a temporary basis. This, despite conflicting results, does not on balance appear to be limited in capacity as a result of aging, but response time is increased, and in addition the rate of scanning (that is, 'looking'; through the temporary information store), does seem to decrease with age (Madden and Nebes, 1980). Both these factors may have complicated research in this area. Certainly Smith and Fullerton (1981) felt that there was no empirical evidence to suggest short-term memory is more vulnerable in aged people.

Differences do occur in recall from episodic memory. It appears that aging affects the acquisition of new information for storage in memory, either because of a less efficient use of encoding strategies, or as a result of retrieval problems. There also seems to be evidence for an age-related difference in

Figure 1.2: Memory

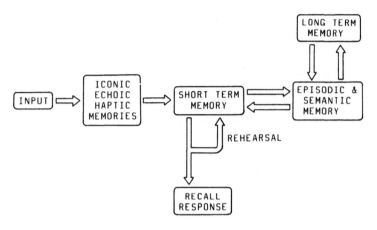

organisation of memory, linked to changes in processing and storage. Semantic memory may reflect a functional adaptation, in that certain aspects of semantic organisation are preferred. For example, older subjects are more likely to store whole propositions, and an increasing number of syntagmatic associations. Burke and Light (1981) found the latter to be true on word association tasks, although both older and younger still used more paradigmatic responses in absolute terms (such as 'cat' in response to 'dog' rather than 'barks' in response to the same cue). The relevance of such changes in semantic organisation for clinical work with language-impaired older adults needs to be carefully considered. The older population seem to be more rigid in their approach to new information, and this well-evidenced fact may well have affected performance in some of the experiments looking at memory via rather artificial tasks. Many other variables within the testing situation may affect results, such as stimulus mode and intensity, presentation, attention and sociocultural factors. Such variables are likely also to be relevant to clinical rehabilitation work.

Attention skills. These are important considerations in both research and clinical work. There are many anecdotal reports of the poorer attention skills of elderly people, but there remains a need to investigate this aspect of aging more objectively. One attempt to study levels of auditory stimulus necessary for speech discrimination did suggest the influence of attention. Posner and Ventry (1977) found that subjects rated 56 dB as most comfortable, but gained optimal comprehension at a lower level of 37 dB, the authors attributing this to the increased attention level needed at the lowered intensity. It is generally accepted that ill health, and specifically brain damage (for example after CVA), do affect attention.

Learning effectiveness is influenced by memory, attention, reinforcement, interference, pacing, adjustment, perception and creativity (Knox, 1981). A further factor is the method or technique employed in teaching new information, such as direct instruction, modelling and practice. It has already been stated that older people demonstrate increased rigidity in dealing with new information, and this may well mean that the techniques employed successfully with younger adults may not be appropriate or most effective with an older population.

Intelligence is a controversial concept, that has been studied by numerous researchers. The balance of opinion seems to be that there is a constant or 'crystallised' IQ, but that a decline occurs with age in 'fluid' IQ (Cattell, 1943). That is, the older individual is less able to adapt to new input, but retains well-rehearsed skills. It may well be that functionally useful abilities are retained, and the contracted life-style of many older people means that they are unlikely to be asked to cope with too much novel information — unless they are unlucky enough to be asked to take part in experimental studies!

Williams, Denney and Schadler (1983) looked at how elderly adults perceived their own memory and problem-solving skills. They felt their memories were less effective, as a result of lowered activity levels, too little contact with the information to be remembered, too little practice, irrelevant and unimportant material, and their own expectations of memory change. However, they felt that their problem-solving abilities were increased, as a result of experience, taking more time, and good health. These views contradict the generally accepted empirical evidence that elderly people are less good at problem solving. It seems likely that their perceptions related to solving everyday problems, and that aged individuals develop a more practical approach to problems.

Psychosocial changes

Allman (1982) suggested that it is the cognitive representation of objective reality that is more important to behaviour than objectively measured facts. Psychological aging refers to the individual's adaptive capacities within his life situation and potential. It will therefore be affected by personality and by life experience — both of those events in common with their cohorts (such as war and economic depressions) and those specific to themselves (such as marriage and occupational history). Past adaptations to life changes will influence how people approach 'becoming and being old'. Many elderly people view old age in a highly negative way (often more so than do middle-aged people) and depression is common among older age groups, a fact that may indicate the adjustment problems many face in accepting the changes that age brings.

Social aging was described by Idris Williams (1985) as a 'composite index to an individual's performance in social roles'. Throughout life people enter a sequence of social roles. Certain patterns of roles tend to reflect stages of development, and relate to age-linked norms of behaviour — whether a person is seen as 'too young' or 'too old' for certain activities. Socio-economic and cultural background will also affect how individuals perceive their roles in life, and their status. Bengston, Kasschan and Ragan (1977) found, for example, that lower classes perceived themselves as 'old' more readily than did higher status subjects. In the United States, similarly, non-whites saw themselves as old at an earlier age than did whites.

Extensive social adjustments must be made as roles alter or are lost, for example on retirement, or when children leave home. All too often no substitute role is found, and the person faces a crisis of social identity. Dolen and Beavison (1982) asked how their subjects viewed their participation in certain roles and activities. They found that chronological age *per se* was not useful in predicting social-cognitive abilities, but that the range of, and amount of involvement in, their social lives was useful. They did, however, find a slight but significant diminution in social activity past 75 years old, and — perhaps surprisingly — that men occupied more roles than did women in this age group. There are those elderly people who are unable to maintain social equilibrium, and therefore require some degree of protection and care. It may be that this relates to such factors as poor housing and low income levels, or to availability of social contacts.

It must not be assumed that in physiological, sensori-perceptual, cognitive or other areas, old age is a common experience. The heterogeneity of this population must be acknowledged, and more than lip service must be paid to it.

DIRECT EFFECTS OF AGING ON COMMUNICATION

Those age-related changes that have so far been discussed may all influence the communication process, as can be seen by Figure 1.1. The following sections describe the specific effects of the aging process on communication.

Comprehension

Among the aspects of mental performance that influence language comprehension can be numbered speech discrimination, response time, attention, memory, distractability and redundancy (Cohen, 1979). It is reasonable therefore to suppose that comprehension ability will reflect age-related changes in these aspects.

However, it is important to recognise what process is being studied; for example, Davis (1984) points out that hearing is a prerequisite for auditory comprehension, but not for the *process* of auditory comprehension.

Knowledge of word meanings appears to be well retained, as has been evidenced by word recognition and definition tasks. Sentence comprehension also appears to be largely intact, except in the case of unusual semantic or complex syntactic forms, but the comprehension of connected prose is considered less efficient by some researchers. Cohen (1979), for instance, used a sentence verification task to conclude that elderly subjects needed more explicit data, and have a differential impairment in processing implicit meaning. Belmore (1981) looked at this so-called 'semantic deficit theory' and found no significant difference in making inferences due to age. Another complex structure that has been studied relates to humour comprehension. Schaier and Cicirelli (1976) looked at this, and found appreciation of verbal humour increased with age until a 'watershed' was reached, beyond which the joke was not understood. Sentence context and redundant information do appear to facilitate comprehension in older subjects (Cohen and Faulkner, 1983).

In summary, it seems that aging may influence language comprehension, but that age *per se* does not functionally impair this ability. However, language testing, which places artificial demands on the testee, may reveal apparent deficits in older adults. This problem will be considered in greater detail in Chapter 2.

Expressive language

Expressive language may be affected by reaction time, memory, attention and intellectual aspects of mental performance. Vocabulary seems to be quite consistent, although several authors stress that passive vocabulary (tested by word recognition tasks) is constant but there is some decline in active vocabulary, that is those words used spontaneously. Bowles and Poon (1985) comment on mild word finding difficulty reported by older people, which — adopting a psycholinguistic stance — they attribute to a failure to access the lexical network via the semantic (but with an intact lexical network). This they showed by providing definitions and requesting subjects to produce the target word, a task performed less well by older subjects. Walker (1984) found semantic naming errors (such as 'boy' for 'girl') to be typical of the expressive language of older people.

Obler and Albert (1981b) looked at the written discourse of elderly people, and commented on a slower generation of concepts allied to an increased elaborateness of syntax. Fewer themes and fewer sentences were used, but there was a tendency — also noted by others — to use more words when fewer would allow effective transmission. Another frequent observation in relation to discourse production is that output is slowed with more hesitations and interjections, but empirical evidence for this is mixed. Cohen (1979) did not find sentence production to be affected in terms of speed or grammaticality, except on a story retelling task. However, Walker (1984) found that normal age changes were typified by phrase structure errors, such as omission of the definite or indefinite article from the noun phrase, or of the auxiliary verb from the verb phrase.

Despite the changes in expressive language that occur with age, it may be that older individuals are in some situations more effective 'oral transmitters' than are younger. Mergler and Faust (1984–85) looked at story telling, because of its link with elderly people in stereotype. They found that some quality, which they did not attempt to define, of older speakers did help listeners to remember more of a story presented in the narrative style. Certainly elderly people are functionally able to remain effective users of language, in the absence of any pathology, despite differences when compared with younger adults.

Speech production

Speech production is affected by physiological and anatomical changes in respiratory, phonatory, resonating and articulatory systems. Such alterations may be compounded by less efficient sensory feedback mechanisms, needed to amend and refine certain vocal tract gestures. Meyerson (1976) gives an overview of the effects of these factors on speech. In addition to 'normal' age changes there is an increased risk that elderly people may suffer respiratory, muscular or joint disorders that would further affect speech. Ryan and Burk (1974) studied the speech of older subjects and found five parameters that best predicted age — these were slowed rate, voice tremor, laryngeal tension, air loss and imprecise consonants.

Rate

Vowel duration increases with age and may contribute to a slower rate of speech. Benjamin (1982) also found a longer Voice Onset Time in older speakers, and that they tended to use durational changes in order to indicate stress more than did younger speakers. Ramig (1983), one of the few researchers to have looked at the 'physiologically aged' (based on measures of heart rate, blood pressure, percentage fat and forced vital capacity), found slowing of speech was much more pronounced in the 'poor physiological group' both on speaking and reading tasks.

Articulation

Ryan and Burk (1974) suggested their finding that imprecise consonants were a good predictor of age meant that a minimal dysarthria was a 'normal' part of aging. It seems strange to describe a normal developmental change by using a term that both denotes and connotes disorder. It is likely that research may have been affected by failing to consider the heterogeneity of the over 65-year-old population.

Pitch

Mysak and Hanley (1958) wrote a classic paper on pitch characteristics, describing the progressive increase in fundamental frequency that occurs in men between middle age and 80 years of age, after which pitch becomes more variable. Pitch range however is reduced. Greene (1982) points out that voice changes are more marked in men than in women.

The age-related changes in respiration, phonation, resonance, prosody and articulation are not of themselves sufficient to impair functionally the speaker's intelligibility. Again, however, there is increased risk of disorder which would then overlay the changes due to the aging process itself.

Language use

How language is used, in terms of extralinguistic factors (such as the setting and particular interactants), linguistic (discourse structure and cohesion) and paralinguistic factors (such as intonation, which may serve a linguistic function in some languages; gesture; and other non-verbal aspects) has been described as the study of 'pragmatics'. This has been a focus for research in child language over recent years, and is quite as relevant to the study of older speakers. It has been suggested, at several points in this text, that changes or differences in function represent adaptations to life as an older person, and are not deficits. There is therefore a need for study of pragmatic considerations in older people's communication. One such study was that of Holland (1980) who found that age (and to an even greater extent living environment) contributed to performance on her own test of functional communication — the CADL (Communicative Abilities in Daily Living). She interpreted this to mean that age affected general communication and not just language *per se*. It seems likely that the way in which an individual uses language (both verbal and non-verbal) is affected by cognitive and psychosocial changes.

In summary, it is generally accepted that aging affects language and communication. There may be direct changes due to alterations in the central nervous system (there is a suggestion, for example, that hemispheric lateralisation increases, e.g. Obler, Woodward and Albert, 1984) or to the anatomical structures necessary for speech. Sensori-perceptual and cognitive changes will further affect communication. Aging thus results not in a defective ability to communicate, but in a different system. It is only when a pathological condition overlays the effect of aging that disorder will result, or when the social environment creates external barriers to effective communication.

CLINICAL IMPLICATIONS

When considering the effect of aging on the various parameters of communicative behaviour, most crucially the clinician must remember that it is not age as such that matters, but the degree of aging experienced by an individual patient. An important

Table 1.1: Common causes of communication difficulties in elderly people

Communication level	Corresponding disorder	Common causes
Sensory input	Hearing loss	Presbyacusis
		Occupation related
	Visual impairment	Glaucoma
		Cataract
Comprehension	Dysphasia	CVA
	(aphasia)	Trauma
Cognition		Tumour
		Infection
Expression	Dementia	Multi-infarct
		Alzheimer's disease
Voluntary motor	Dyspraxia	CVA
programming	(apraxia)	
Motor output	Dysarthria	CVA
	(anarthria)	Respiratory disease
		Ca. larynx
	Dysphonia	Parkinson's disease
	(aphonia)	Iatrogenic
Opportunity and		Depression
motivation		Institutionalisation
		Isolation

THE AGING PROCESS

need in the clinic is for more reliable and detailed norms relating to the communicative behaviour of the aged population. Until it is known exactly how aging affects communication, it is impossible to be sure what is being assessed and treated. A 'deterioration' has been found on test scores when aphasia batteries have been administered to elderly subjects who appear normal outside the clinic (Walker, 1982). This suggests that new norms are needed, or clinicians may find they are assessing and treating age!

However, the elderly population do face an increased risk of suffering communication difficulty. Some of the disorders that may affect communication, and that are not uncommon among older population groups, are outlined in Table 1.1. In an unpublished survey of patients presenting in a Speech Therapy Clinic for elderly people (Moon, 1984) the most common causes of communication disorders were cerebrovascular accident (CVA), dementia, and Parkinson's disease. Dementia is discussed in more detail in Chapter 4, but it is worth considering CVA and Parkinson's disease briefly at this point. There are numerous fuller texts available on both conditions, and the following discussion is not intended as a comprehensive outline.

Cerebrovascular accident

A cerebrovascular accident or stroke is an acute disturbance of cerebral function causing death, or disability lasting more than 24 hours. CVA may be due to cerebral infarction or cerebral haemorrhage. The former refers to the blockage of a blood vessel feeding part of the brain, which causes the blood flow to fall below the critical level necessary to maintain the tissue viability (Clifford Rose and Capildeo, 1981). Cerebral haemorrhage refers to bleeding into the brain caused by the rupture of a blood vessel or an aneurysm. The disability that results will depend on the area(s) of cerebral tissue that are affected, both in terms of the nature of the disability and in severity. Communication disorders that may result (such as aphasia, dyspraxia and dysarthria) will be discussed more fully in Chapter 2; although it must be remembered that they rarely occur in isolation, and rehabilitation will be affected by the other sequelae of stroke such as motor or sensori-perceptual disorders.

16

If the disability lasts for less than 24 hours the patient is said to have had a transient ischaemic attack (TIA). There is a further group of patients whose disability lasts more than 24 hours but fully recovers within, at most, one month. In order to distinguish this population from those who suffer a completed stroke, the term Reversible Ischaemic Neurological Deficit (RIND) is used.

Stroke can occur at any age, but the incidence rises rapidly with age. Clifford Rose and Capildeo (1981) cite an annual incidence of 9 per 1000 people aged 65–74; 20 in the 75–84 year old group; and 40 in the over 85 age group. The mortality from stroke doubles with each decade after the age of 40 years, but this may be due to the fact that older people are more likely both to have other serious illness, and to suffer complications such as bronchopneumonia.

Parkinson's disease

Parkinsonism is a term that includes a number of disease processes, generally classified as degenerative disorders of the nervous system, associated with a depletion of brain dopamine which implicates the subcortical structures and substantia nigra in particular. The majority of cases are labelled idiopathic (i.e. have no known cause), but a proportion are attributable to infective, vascular, iatrogenic (i.e. drug related), and other causes. The Parkinsonian syndrome is characterised by a triad of physical signs — tremor, muscular rigidity, and bradykinesia. There is often a typical disorder of gait known as 'marche à petits pas'. Considerable time has gone into studying the relationship of Parkinson's disease and dementia. This is discussed further in Chapter 4.

There may be a speech disorder in as many as 50 per cent of sufferers (Oxtoby, 1982), which presents as a dysarthria characterised by breathiness, monotony, altered rate (often festinance occurs), initiation difficulty and imprecise articulation. Not all symptoms will be present in any one person, and some researchers have queried whether there is in fact poor articulation or whether this is the effect of dysprosody (e.g. Scott, Caird and Williams, 1985). General approaches to assessment and treatment of dysarthria will be discussed in Chapter 2, but it seems to be accepted that an intensive therapy routine, with subsequent follow-up courses, is particularly useful in the case of Parkinson's disease patients (Robertson and Thomson, 1984).

Medical treatment is largely by drug therapy, although rarely surgical intervention to alleviate rigidity and tremor is undertaken. Drug therapy involves use of either anticholinergic or dopaminergic therapy (usually L-dopa with a peripheral decarboxylase inhibitor). Side effects are common.

Perkin (1986) describes Parkinsonism as relatively common, affecting some 1 per cent of the population over the age of 50; more sufferers between 61 and 70 at onset, than in younger or older age groups.

Aging leads to changes in communicative ability that mean specialised intervention is needed when an older person suffers a communicative disorder. Some such patients will be able to respond to the traditional therapy techniques employed with an adult population, and these will be described briefly in Chapter 2. Others will not be suitable for traditional therapy, and the speech therapist must be flexible and prepared to move away from the medical model of curative treatment. Weiss (1971) offered a three-level approach to working with the communicatively impaired elderly. The first two levels — diagnostic evaluation and direct therapy — can be described as traditional, whereas the third level aimed to involve lay and professional carers in supporting the therapy undertaken by the clinicians. It will be argued in subsequent chapters that this, and other indirect approaches to the management of elderly patients, may prove to be a more realistic use of clinical time and, most importantly, lead to better and more effective patient care.

2

Traditional Approaches to Assessment and Therapy

Direct or Traditional Therapy may be viewed as those remedial activities which are undertaken with an individual, or group of individuals, which focus upon a specific area of acquired disability. Indirect Therapy approaches are those remedial or supportive activities aimed at an individual or group of individuals, but undertaken through family, professional carers and/or the environment, when direct therapy is either inappropriate or insufficient to achieve the person's full potential for rehabilitation. Ideally, therefore, both direct and indirect therapy should be considered for each patient.

Figure 2.1 indicates some of the management decisions with which the speech therapist will be faced, and provides an outline of both direct and indirect courses of action that may be taken. Following the initial referral a case history is taken, and the appropriate assessment — formal or informal — carried out. While it can be useful to make a diagnosis — Wertz, LaPointe and Rosenbek (1984) stress its crucial nature in implying prognosis and management — there are times when diagnosis is unclear, and then a course of 'diagnostic therapy' can be instigated. If there is doubt, a diagnosis should be delayed for the same reasons that it can be useful, that is, that it will imply prognosis and suggest management which may then prove to be mistaken. Labelling tends to stick, and it is commonly found that people react to the label rather than to the individual. Perhaps the most dangerous mistake that a speech therapist working with elderly people can make is in wrongly differentially diagnosing dementia and aphasia, a question that will be addressed in greater detail in Chapter 4.

Assessment is followed by the basic management decision as

ASSESSMENT AND THERAPY

Figure 2.1: Referral

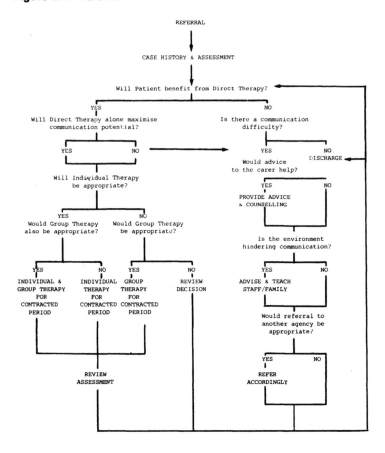

to whether direct therapy would be appropriate, and whether additional indirect therapy is needed instead or as well as the more traditional approach. The actual speech and language disorders found amongst an elderly population are not specific to the aged. The more common conditions will be outlined briefly in terms of assessment and therapy, in order to set the perspective for a discussion of management principles in working with older people.

Those conditions presenting most frequently in an Adult Speech Therapy Clinic are aphasia, dysarthria, dyspraxia and dysphonia. The more traditional approaches to their management will be described, and such direct intervention as may apply to both younger and older adults, in the absence of complicating factors.

INDIVIDUAL APPROACHES TO MANAGEMENT

Aphasia

Aphasia refers to a disruption of language as a result of brain damage. It is multi-modal, affecting auditory comprehension, verbal expression, reading and writing. 'The symptom complexes . . . vary as a function of the location and extent of brain damage, and these variations are evident in differing patterns and degrees of impairment in linguistic performance' (Davis and Holland, 1981). Figure 2.2 shows the main areas of the dominant cerebral hemisphere, damage to which results in aphasic symptoms. The most common cause of aphasia is cerebrovascular accident.

Figure 2.2: The brain — lateral view of the left hemisphere

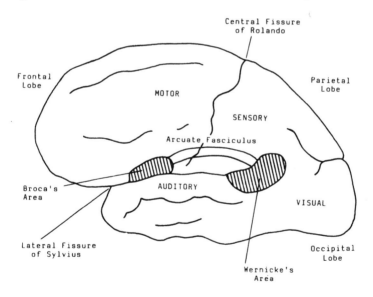

While in practice the terms aphasia and dysphasia are used interchangeably, the latter denotes a degree of language impairment, and the former a total loss of language ability.

Confusion between spoken versions of dysphasia and dysphagia in North America has led many therapists to adopt 'aphasia' as a generic term — as has been done in this text.

Assessment

Aphasia tests have existed for some time, and have at times been taken too literally. Emerick and Hatten (1974) say 'It is dreadfully easy to be seduced by a particular diagnostic tool to the point that we come to see aphasia and the aphasic solely through a test . . . it is worth at least as much time to appreciate the impact of aphasia upon an individual's humanity'. Table 2.1 shows some of the more commonly used assessments, most of which look at language via a multi-modal approach. The recent increase in attempts to assess functional communication skills has been applauded by most clinicians working with an aphasic population, and particularly with older patients. This is illustrated by the fact that on conventional aphasia batteries there is a deterioration in scores for elderly subjects which does not of necessity reflect a functionally significant communication impairment (Walker, 1984). Thus therapists must be able to

Table 2.1: Language tests in common usage

A. Language Batteries	
i. Boston Diagnostic Aphasia Examination	Goodglass and Kaplan (1972)
ii. The Language Modalities Test for Aphasia	Wepman and Jones (1961)
iii. The Minnesota Test for Differential Diagnosis of Aphasia	Schuell (1965)
iv. Neurosensory Centre Comprehensive Examination of Aphasia	Spreen and Benton (1969)
v. Porch Index of Communicative Ability	Porch (1973)
vi. Western Aphasia Battery	Kertesz (1982)
vii. Aphasia Language Performance Scales	Keenan and Brassell (1975)
viii. Appraisal of Language Disturbance	Emerick (1971)
ix. Examining of Aphasia	Eisenson (1954)
x. Orzeck Aphasia Evaluation	Orzeck (1964)
xi. Sklar Aphasia Scale	Sklar (1966)
xii. An Aphasia Screening Test	Whurr (1974)
B. Functional Assessments	
i. Functional Communication Profile	Taylor Sarno (1969)
ii. Communicative Abilities in Daily Living (CADL)	Holland (1980)
iii. Edinburgh Functional Communication Profile	Skinner *et al.* (1984)

separate the proportion of behaviour due to a primary disorder from that due to the aging process. It is crucial that the therapist is sure what an assessment is actually measuring.

Therapy

Aphasia therapy has been traditionally based on a stimulus–facilitation–response–feedback approach, such as that advocated by Schuell. This is based on a multi-modal orientation, with hierarchies of complexity within each mode. According to Walker and Williams (1980) the principles of aphasia therapy are first that each stimulus should elicit a response without struggle, at the highest level of the patient's ability. Secondly, responses should be reinforced by feedback, verbal reward, other modalities and self correction. Thirdly, meaningful and verbally useful materials should be used, and fourthly, there should be a gradual elimination of clues toward latent spontaneous language or a new response. The final two principles are that gross sensory discrimination should lead on to finer distinctions, and simple tasks to more complex and abstract ones.

Table 2.2: Aphasia therapy techniques

i. Melodic Intonation Therapy (MIT)	Sparks, Helm and Albert (1974)
ii. Promoting Aphasic's Communicative Effectiveness (PACE)	Davies and Wilcox (1981)
iii. Deblocking	Weigl (1968)
iv. Syntax Stimulation Programme	Helm-Estabrooks and Albert (1980)
v. Visual Action Therapy	Helm-Estabrooks, Fitzpatrick and Barresi (1982)
vi. Visual Communication Therapy	Gardner *et al.* (1976)
vii. Voluntary Control of Involuntary Utterances	Helm and Barresi (1980)
viii. Semantic, Oppositional and Rhyming Retrieval Training (SORRT)	Logue and Dixon (1979)
ix. Lexical Focus	Linebaugh (1983)
x. Verbal Modelling Technique	Cooper and Rigrodosky (1979)
xi. Intersystemic Reorganisation	Luria (1970)
xii. Thought Centred Therapy	Wepman (1976)

Table 2.2 lists some of the more specific techniques that have been devised for use with aphasia patients, usually aiming to

restore specific functions — as do Melodic Intonation Therapy and Visual Action Therapy. Functional approaches such as PACE (Promoting Aphasic's Communicative Effectiveness; Davis and Wilcox, 1981), have been valuable, as they recognise that communicative competence cannot be directly predicted from measures of linguistic functioning. They also allow for the different experiences of individual patients.

Therapy will be affected by such factors as sensory losses, learning ability and experience. Health and environment will also be influences, as will the expectations held by patient, family and therapist. Age *per se* has not been found to be a major factor in recovery from aphasia although it may influence the type of aphasia and — as will be discussed later — some of the practicalities of therapy.

There has been much debate about the effectiveness of speech therapy with aphasic patients. It is outside the scope of this text, but it is important that the different techniques of therapy are studied, rather than all approaches lumped together under the umbrella of 'Therapy'. It is often true that techniques are tried, but not tested.

Once therapy has achieved its potential, it is increasingly seen as part of the speech therapist's role to assist adjustment to the residual impairment. Thus, the major objective of therapy with aphasics is, as Wertz said '. . . to maximise and maintain communication skills for independent living, emotional adjustment and effective environmental contact'.

Dyspraxia

Darley (1969) defined dyspraxia of speech as

An articulatory disorder resulting from impairment, as a result of brain damage, of the capacity to program the positioning of speech musculature and the sequencing of muscle movements for the volitional production of phonemes. No significant weakness, slowness or incoordination in reflex and automatic acts. Prosodic alterations may be associated with the articulatory problem, perhaps in compensation for it.

Total lack of ability voluntarily to produce speech is apraxia.

Assessment

The assessment of dyspraxia is complicated by the frequent co-occurrence of dyphasia. Wertz *et al.* (1984) suggest that samples are taken of language, speech, non-verbal oral movements, limb gestures and intelligence. Diagnosis stems from the recognition of a specific pattern of speech behaviours, rather than from any single symptom.

Therapy

Treatment is the 'structured relearning of skilled speech movements'. The patient must learn careful planning, execution, evaluation and self correction. One of the basic premises for therapy with dyspraxics is to utilise the intact tactile—kinaesthetic feedbacks to compensate for the lack of control. It may be that older people are less able to develop this skill, because of less-efficient learning abilities, and decreased sensitivity via all sensory modalities (Franks, 1982). In addition, physical working capacity may be reduced, which will affect response to taxing, repetitive drills (Davis and Baggs, 1984). However, as in aphasia, age *per se* is not the major factor in recovery or management. The goal of therapy is to reinstate as much speech as possible, but to make use of alternative communication modes when necessary. The aim of adjustment to residual losses as a focus of therapy would apply, as to other patients.

Dysarthria

As Rosenbek and LaPointe (1981) state: 'The idea of a unitary dysarthria is being refined to the more inclusive view of the dysarthrias'. The dysarthrias are a group of related motor speech disorders, which are due to a disturbance of muscular control necessary for the production of intelligible speech. Anarthria is the extreme at which no speech is possible. The disturbance may stem from central or peripheral impairment, and a wide variety of neuropathologies can cause these conditions. Elderly people face an increased risk of suffering certain of these conditions, such as cerebrovascular accident (CVA) or Parkinson's disease. In addition, there are natural changes as a person ages, which some feel may masquerade as a mild motor speech disorder.

Assessment

Diagnosis stems from a full history, and both informal and standardised assessments. Traditionally, motor speech processes have been split into areas of respiration, phonation, resonance, articulation and prosody — each of which is evaluated in isolation, and in relation to the other areas. It is often these inter-relationships, or the co-ordination of actions which is affected.

Most formal assessments base on perceptual evaluation, such as the Frenchay Dysarthria Assessment (Enderby, 1983) and the Dysarthria Profile (Robertson, 1982), but there is an increasing use of instrumentation to allow more objective and precise measurement. Rosenbek and LaPointe do point out that individuals can be easier or harder to understand than one would predict from specific tests of function, and therefore perhaps the most crucial aspect to assess is intelligibility within connected speech.

While much attention has focused on attempts to assess the functional impact of aphasia, this has not tended to be a priority in assessing dysarthric patients. Particularly with older people a formal assessment looking at the influence of the disorder on their daily life, allied to the more objective assessment of specific muscular function and co-ordination, may be useful.

Therapy

The aim of therapy is to improve the physiological support for speech. However, the tedious drills that this necessitates, alongside the increased likelihood of coexisting pathologies and of fatigue, mean that this aim may be less appropriate for some elderly patients. Compensatory techniques and strategies can be taught, such as slowing rate, pacing and altering pitch.

Patient co-operation is essential if therapy is to be effective. Speech (and language) therapy is an active process, and thus demands active participation from the client. Full explanations and counselling, with relevant and realistic goal planning, will encourage this co-operation. However, it is often the experience of clinicians working with aged dysarthric patients that they are ready to accept low levels of intelligibility. While explanations may gently persuade some to participate in a trial period of therapy, it is, of course, ultimately the right of the patient to refuse. This right must be acknowledged.

Dysphonia

Dysphonia is a disorder of voice production, while aphonia refers to a total loss of voice. Voice production can be considered as a continuum from unstrained clear production through dysphonia, which may be due to pathology, misuse or neurosis, to aphonia.

Assessment

Evaluation by the speech therapist follows a medical examination, which should reveal whether there is a functional or organic cause for the dysphonia, although these two causative factors should be viewed not as discrete aetiologies, but along a continuum. A full case history is important, to establish the problem in terms of onset, cause, duration, variation and presentation.

Testing includes both subjective and objective measures of respiration, phonation (pitch, volume and quality) and resonance. As Boone (1977) stresses, the clinician must also be familiar with the patient and his feelings about the disorder.

Therapy

Voice therapy may be undertaken as the procedure of choice, or as an adjunct to other treatments. In the former case, it may be used to attempt to alleviate a laryngeal pathology (such as nodules due to misuse of the voice) prior to considering other treatment, or as a compensatory approach (for example, after paralysis), or in non-organic dysphonia. In co-ordination with other treatments it may precede or follow an operation or use of a prosthesis in order to introduce and maintain good vocal habits, or occur in combination with other treatments such as psychology or physiotherapy.

The first step will be for the therapist and patient to establish realistic aims and target vocal behaviours. There are changes in voice production due to the aging process, and it may be difficult to decide what is a true dysphonia in an elderly patient, and subsequently what constitutes a realistic aim. It may also be that both the older person and the medical profession are more ready to accept a degree of vocal change, so that fewer elderly patients are referred with dysphonia as the primary communication difficulty.

One exception is in the person who presents with dysphonia

due to laryngeal carcinoma, the incidence of which rises with age. While radiotherapy and chemotherapy will often be the preferred treatment, if the patient's condition necessitates a total or partial laryngectomy, pre- and postoperative support and voice restoration therapy will be needed, as for a laryngectomee of any age. There are excellent texts available on the management of the laryngectomee.

Dysphagia

Dysphagia is defined as a disorder of swallowing, and has become an important aspect of the speech therapist's work over recent years. While it does not strictly speaking fall into the category of specific communication disorders, it should be mentioned as a disorder with which the speech therapist may be directly involved.

Successful intervention should be a team effort, whether the dysphagia has a peripheral (as in cases of damage to the IX, X or XIIth cranial nerves, which can occur, for example, during a laryngectomy) or a neurological cause (as may be found in motor neurone disease, or CVA, for instance). Again there are excellent texts on this subject, covering assessment and rehabilitation (e.g. Logemann, 1983).

Assessment

Assessment involves both bedside and instrumental observation, with more and more hospitals establishing dysphagia clinics. 'Bedside evaluation' attempts to get the patient's opinion, and to gain an overall picture of the difficulty they experience, and whether it is at the oral, pharyngeal or oesophageal level. It is not always possible to define properly the difficulty, and cine x-ray techniques or videofluoroscopy can be necessary. Aspiration, for example, may occur without being obvious from a bedside assessment, but will show up on x-ray.

Therapy

If the problem is at the oral or oesophageal phase the patient may be able to respond to direct instruction, aiming to modify behaviours. The involvement of the team is important as other disciplines can contribute — the occupational therapist, for example, may suggest feeding aids. The family should be involved as much as possible, and be advised both on how to feed, or how to help the patient feed, and on dietary needs. Both patient and family may need help and support to cope with the social side of a feeding disorder.

There will be those who cannot achieve oral feeding, and will need to be fitted with a nasogastric tube. This is not necessarily the end of the need for the speech therapist to be involved, and she may continue to play an important role in reassessing advising and supporting the patient and others.

GROUP THERAPY

The therapy approaches discussed in the preceding section have been aimed at individual patient contact. However, group therapy for communication disorders has become an increasingly popular mode of treatment, attempting to bridge the often startling gap between individual therapy and returning to life in the community without rehabilitative support. There are many reasons why group therapy can be beneficial, both in terms of speech–language rehabilitation, and in helping the psychological adjustment necessary to cope with a residual impairment in communication.

Groups provide a more natural social setting, which compared with individual work in the clinic, can be relatively informal and relaxed. Members realise that others suffer similar disabilities, and are also given the opportunity to form relationships with people who accept them as they are now. Often 'old' friends and family find it hard not to continually, and indeed understandably, draw attention back to how the person once was. Members can meet within a group on an equal basis, and escape from the situation in which they are the 'helped' and others the 'helpers'. Feelings can be shared and expressed without fear of judgement, and thus members may gain confidence to experiment without fear of failure.

Communication impairment often leads to feelings of isolation. This is true whether the communication disorder is primary (as in the case of aphasia) or secondary to an overlying condition (as in hearing impairment). Often the experience gained in an organised group can help an individual to relate better outside its protective walls. It is often said that a group reduces the patient's dependency upon the therapist. This may or may not be true. Many group members will continue to interact through the therapist, and it may be necessary to plan specifically to encourage them to look to each other for support.

Any group is only as good as its members, but should in total be greater than the sum of its parts. Selection of members is therefore crucial, and consideration should be given to their ability to fit into the group, as well as to individual needs. No one member should demand too great a share of the group's time. Each member must be prepared to show interest in others, and to assume some responsibility for the group's functioning. At the same time, the therapist must recognise that there is no guarantee that the members will gel just because they match the selection criteria. The therapist's role is to direct and encourage, rather than to dominate, and to ensure that all members participate, and take on as much responsibility as their handicaps realistically allow.

Obviously many decisions will depend upon the aims of the group. These aims will determine membership criteria, location, frequency and the size of the group. For example, a group for the confused will need to have a higher staff–patient ratio, and to meet more frequently than will a group for high level aphasic patients.

Most of the documented cases of group therapy, in the field of speech and language rehabilitation, have been with aphasics, although there are examples of groups for dysarthric patients, laryngectomees and others. The consensus has been that such groups are beneficial, but it may be that the benefits are greatest in enabling members better to adjust to residual disabilities, rather than in terms of specific speech and language recovery.

MANAGEMENT PRINCIPLES: WORKING WITH ELDERLY PEOPLE

Some of the main disorders have been discussed briefly. However, it is important to consider how assessment and therapy may need to be adapted when working with elderly patients.

Assessment

The major difficulty to be faced in assessing speech and

language disorders in elderly people is that many tests were devised within a 'non-developmental, pathology oriented context' (Botwinick, 1973), or were standardised on younger populations. They often do not provide norms for older subjects despite the fact that age-related changes in communication are known to exist. This means that the validity and reliability of tests when used with an elderly population will be suspect. The tests themselves also age, and may become less and less valid. Furthermore, overgeneralising tests from their country of origin to other countries can present difficulties, as has been found by many British therapists making use of American assessment materials, for example.

Botwinick also talks of the need to consider cautiousness, expectations of negative feedback, and the extension of risk-avoiding behaviour within an assessment situation. Test anxiety and caution in responding seem to be greater in older people (Chown, 1977). If attempts are made to establish norms for an elderly population, adjustments in the materials and manner of presentation might be woven into the standardisation procedure, in order to remove possible biases due to sensori-perceptual, motor and other changes resulting from developmental processes. However, the presentation of existing tests

Table 2.3: Problems encountered in testing elderly patients

TEST VARIABLES	Inappropriate norms	Standardised on younger adults
	Materials — content and presentation	Failure to consider sensory losses
	Length	Fatiguability
CLINICIAN	Low expectations Stereotype of elderly	
PATIENT	Reaction to testing situation	Lack of motivation Anxiety Caution Low expectations Poor cooperation
	Complicating factors (multiple pathologies common)	Confusion Anxiety Memory loss Hearing loss
ENVIRONMENT	Institutionalisation effects (differential diagnostic factor)	

cannot be adapted without compromising further their validity and reliability. Thus, normal aging may complicate testing procedure and the interpretation of results. Walker (1984) summarised the complicating factors as being the lack of appropriate tests and test norms, contradictory evidence in differentiating between normal and pathological, and the possibility of premorbid deterioration in communication. Table 2.3 suggests some of the problems encountered when testing the elderly patient.

In addition to these problems in assessing elderly people, there are also clinician-based factors of acceptance of stereotypes, and lowered expectations of elderly patients. As Schaie and Schaie (1977) point out, the therapist must, as well as considering such factors as the length of the test and spacing of stressful questions, be aware of and sensitive to personality and culture. It may be, too, that the rules or criteria used in assessing younger adults' ability to benefit from therapy should not be generalised to older age groups.

Therapy

Patient variables

In working with elderly people, the first priority must be to ensure such factors as sensory losses have been 'treated' whenever possible, whether by the provision of glasses and/or hearing aids, or by environmental manipulation (such as changes in the lighting, minimising background noise and so on). Learning effectiveness will also influence therapy, and is affected by memory, reinforcement, interference, pacing and adjustment. Knox (1981) goes on to stress that the older population will need to set their own pace, and when possible to be actively involved in selecting and organising activities. This may well improve motivation. If learning is 'enhanced by satisfactory adjustment to the environment' as Knox states, it could have important implications for working with the institutionalised elderly population.

Sensory losses, learning ability, experience and environment may alter with age, and thus the therapist can attempt to compensate for changes, by altering the number and type of materials used, the length and frequency of sessions, the number of repetitions for which to aim, and the time spent helping the patient to see the value of treatment (Rosenbek and LaPointe, 1981). Slowed reaction time suggests material presentation should be slowed, and a longer time allowed for response. Fatiguability, as well as leading to shorter sessions, should be dealt with in part by ensuring that sessions are not scheduled after other tiring activities, such as physiotherapy. This can be a major difficulty if older clients are expected to attend as out-patients and have to endure long and frustrating ambulance journeys in order to reach the clinic. Tompkins, Marshall and Phillips (1980) looked at the question of schedul-

Table 2.4: The effects of drugs on communication

Drug	Possible effects on communication
Anticonvulsants	
(e.g. phenytoin; Tegretol)	Cerebellar dysarthria
Neuromuscular blockers	Dysarthria
L-Dopa	Articulatory effects
	Orofacial dyskinesia
	Higher mental functions affected
Anti-anxiety/sedatives	
1. Benzodiazepines	Reading impaired
(e.g. diazepam)	More inaudible or unintelligible
	words and remarks
	Recent memory impaired
	More incomplete utterances
2. Sedatives	Slurred speech
(e.g. methyprylone)	Word finding and order affected
	(may at extreme present as jargon)
Antidepressants and mood stabilisers	
1. Tricyclics	Disorientation
(e.g. amitriptyline)	Memory impairment
	Difficulty with word retrieval and
2. MAOIs	in expressing thoughts (presenting
(e.g. phenelzine)	in dysfluency)
	Dysarthria and scanning speech
3. Lithium salts	Decreased salivation
Anti-psychotics	
1. Phenothiazines	Less spontaneity and more
(e.g. chlorpromazine)	circumscription in speech
	Secondary Parkinsonism (with
2. Thioxanthenes	characteristic effects on speech)
(e.g. Clopenthixol)	Tardive dyskinesia (hyperkinetic
	dysarthria)
3. Butyrophenones	Decreased salivation
(e.g. haloperidol)	

Source: Based on Gawel 'The effects of various drugs on speech'. *British Journal of Disorders of Communication*, 1981, *16*, 51–7.

ing speech and language services, and found that their aphasic subjects' performances were significantly affected by the time of day at which they were assessed.

Clinicians in the United States have had to face the difficulties which come from working with adults who come from very different cultural and racial backgrounds. This is also becoming more noticeable in Great Britain, as immigrants who arrived in the postwar period are now being seen in geriatric departments. Davis and Holland (1981) discuss a 'life cycle' form, which they use to record a patient's personal history, and then relate these personal milestones to the historical events at that time. Such an approach could help the clinician to gain insight into the different experiences of their patients, especially in the case of immigrants. A full case history can also help in planning therapy and choosing materials for assessment and remedial work. Obviously very specific problems will be faced if patients are not English speaking, but cultural differences should be considered even in English-speaking minority groups.

An important patient variable in relation both to assessment and therapy is that individual's drug regime. Table 2.4 indicates the effects of some of the drugs commonly prescribed to the elderly, that may affect communication.

Rosenbek and LaPointe also stress the relevance of this in their work on Motor Speech Disorders (1981), where they describe a patient who presented with hypokinetic dysarthria which immediately resolved upon ceasing to prescribe the drug haloperidol. Obviously, medication is not necessarily stopped because of side effects on communication, as these may be acceptable when weighed against the drug's benefits. Knowledge of the drug regime may, however, influence the decision to offer speech therapy, and how to manage the presenting communication disorder.

The need to consider drug intake is not always clear-cut, particularly in relation to prescribing for elderly people, as various disorders or conditions can lead to problems in following directions relating to drug dosages. Some of these are outlined in Table 2.5, and it is a common and worrying problem particularly when elderly people suffering from memory loss, or another of these complicating conditions, live alone.

Obler and Albert (1981b) support the view of many who feel that elderly people develop strategies to cope with communication changes. They suggest that more knowledge of such factors

Table 2.5: Common problems in drug dosages in the elderly

	Condition	Examples of causes	Problems
1.	Deafness	Presbyacusis	Failure to hear details of timing and dosage
2.	Visual impairment	Glaucoma Cataract	Difficulty reading labels and warnings Difficulty seeing syringe markings
3.	Impaired dexterity	Hemiparesis/ Hemiplegia post CVA	Difficulty opening bottles Difficulty with drops/creams
4.	Depression		Poor co-operation Indifference and apathy to necessary medication
5.	Memory disorder	CVA Dementia	Difficulty with time factors and patterns of dosage Over or under dosage common

Source: Based on I. Felstein 'When drugs are also a problem for the old'. 1985, *Therapy Weekly*, Sept.

might allow the therapist to incorporate these 'normal' strategies into therapy programmes. It may also encourage a more functional approach to their problems, and thus affect motivation.

Clinician variables

Eisdorfer and Stotsky (1977) note the importance of the 'Therapist's technical skills, degree of commitment, utilisation of pragmatic strategies and recognition of environmental influences'. They also refer to the therapist's expectations as being a 'salient issue in treatment'. While they were not specifically talking about the speech-language therapist, these variables seem just as relevant, and are interesting in relation to work by Muller, Code and Mingford (1983). They found therapists working with aphasic patients to be more pessimistic than either patient or spouse — who were equally optimistic. It may be that these lowered expectations influence the therapeutic relationship. Rogers (1961) in his classic work 'On Becoming a Person' discussed this relationship, stressing the need to set aside external frames of reference, such as attitudes towards 'the elderly', in order to allow 'unconditional positive regard' and 'empathy' to extend from therapist to patient.

While it is accepted that the clinician has an important influence on therapy outcome, as Wertz, LaPointe and Rosenbek (1984) point out, clinical education and experience are so variable that they are beyond the scope of discussion.

Type of intervention

The clinician's choice of technique may be an influential factor in the amount of recovery made by the patient, although efficacy studies have tended not to specify techniques. Apart from these methods, while underlying them to a greater or lesser extent, is the general approach. Denney (1981) looked at research into various types of intervention with elderly people and attempted to summarise the findings. She found that modelling was largely effective (although there were some conflicting studies). Direct instruction had been studied, but via methods that Denney felt to be inadequate in both design and reporting. It appears that the elderly benefit less from this than do younger clients, although this may be a function of the complexity of verbal instruction. Feedback is almost impossible to study in isolation, but seems useful in tandem with modelling or direct instruction. The value of practice is also hard to assess, but may be more useful with certain abilities, or if certain types of practice are considered.

Discharge

The question of if and when to discharge a patient of any age, has been a subject for much discussion among speech therapists. It is accepted that there are some patients (and indeed some families of patients) who are resistant to discharge. Langyut, Madison and Weir (1983) looked at this question, and felt that resistance could be due to acquired advantages of therapy, in that it perpetuates the sick role, and relieves the person from risking failure in meeting social responsibilities, and may be part of the coping repertoire of the patient. It does seem that some patients use speech therapy to fulfil social and psycho-emotional needs as well as communicative needs, and those who do seem to are those who have low self-esteem and are unhappy with some facet of their lives. Langyut *et al.* also found that older patients resist discharge more, but that socioeconomic class, sex and the nature of the disorder were also related.

The therapist may foster this resistance if she or he is unable to explain that further recovery is unlikely, and feels a degree of 'guilt' at not having cured the patient. Alen-Buckley, Stevens and Davis (1982), in their brief article, point out that there is often subtle pressure to continue treatment beyond the time when adjustment has reached a good level. However, how this 'good' level of adjustment is defined is impossible to specify, although the role relatives or friends play should never be underestimated. Wertz (1984) makes the point that the patient has needs *after* he has achieved his maximum level of speech and language recovery. He suggests considering input in two phases — the direct rehabilitation role, and subsequently work on helping the person to adjust to the residual communicative handicap.

Contractual agreements at the start of therapy can help to lessen the resistance to discharge, especially if backed up with 'warnings' as to how long remains. Full explanations to the whole family will often be valuable in creating realistic expectations, and thus better adjustment to the communication deficit that remains. It is, however, useful to leave the clinic door ajar, if not open, so that further advice or counsel can be sought when necessary. If, for example, an older person's spouse dies, whoever takes on the caring role may need new advice and explanations.

Wertz mentioned another side to discharge resistance which stems from the therapist who attempts to make too many of the patient's decisions for him. The extreme of this results in Wertz's comment that 'Too often . . . we put patients into treatment when they do not want to be nor should be there'. Nowhere does this seem to be more true than with an elderly population.

BARRIERS TO DIRECT THERAPY

This chapter has focused on direct work with older adults who have a specific speech or language disability, stressing the need to be aware of how the normal aging process may influence test performance and response to therapy. However, there are those patients who would not be suitable for a course of direct therapy, despite the fact that they have a communication difficulty. There is no doubt that there is an increase in the numbers of those who would not benefit from direct rehabilita-

ASSESSMENT AND THERAPY

Table 2.6: Barriers to direct intervention

i.	Insight reduced or absent
ii.	Co-operation poor
iii.	Motivation low
iv.	Attention reduced
v.	Memory loss
vi.	Cognitive impairment
vii.	Learning ability reduced
viii.	Sensory losses (unmanaged)
ix.	Mental illness
x.	Fatiguability
xi.	Some physical illnesses/disorders
xii.	Environmental factors

tion, with increasing age. The reasons or barriers to the person's ability to respond on this level are several and are summarised in Table 2.6.

A major factor is whether the patient has insight into his communication difficulty. If there is no awareness either of the inappropriate nature of his communication attempt, or of the breakdown of the communicative relationship, then the patient will have no reason to co-operate in therapy. Achieving insight may, of itself, be a goal for intervention, but until that goal is reached there can be no formal speech or language work.

Related to this are the factors of co-operation and motivation. Some older patients are inclined to accept their handicaps rather than to participate in a remedial programme, and many are ready to aim less high than would a younger adult perhaps aiming to return to employment. This may be a difficult area, although time spent on offering clear and full explanations can encourage co-operation. Although the choice must rest ultimately with the patient, it is sad when the quality of his life might be improved by a short course of therapy.

Other barriers are attention and memory deficits, both of which intact skills are needed if there is to be any degree of carry over between sessions. The ability to learn new information is altered in elderly people, and this may affect therapeutic attempts to teach compensatory strategies, or to relearn skills, which have in the past been performed subconsciously. Sensory losses may militate against therapy, if they cannot be adequately managed. The existence of mental illness will also be a factor, affecting cognitive and motivational factors. Physical handicap

38

and fatiguability may lead to the decision that direct work would be counterproductive, and alternative communication methods may be considered.

Finally, barriers may exist within the social environment. Institutionalisation will be discussed at length elsewhere, but isolation may also be an obstacle difficult to overcome. It will limit not only opportunity to communicate, but also the possibility of finding a third party to back up any formal therapy between sessions. While volunteers can perform this role, they are not always suitable for work of this nature, and need to be carefully selected and trained.

If one or more of these barriers exist, the decision may be taken that direct intervention is inappropriate, and often this has heralded the end of the speech therapist's involvement. However, the communication problem persists for both patient and carers. In these cases, indirect involvement can be crucial to encourage the person to communicate at the best possible level, and to help him adjust to his degree of handicap. It can also be the deciding factor as to whether a family can cope with a communicatively impaired member. The major difficulty in this indirect approach — working through family, professionals and the environment — is that evaluation of such diverse intervention can be problematic, and there is a danger that indirect work is seen less objectively by the clinician, than is direct therapy. There must be clearly specified aims — be they in relation to patient, family, environment or other professionals — and methods for attaining these goals must be tried and tested.

Weiss (1971) discussed the communicative needs of the aged population, and nicely summarised the role of therapy as 'not so much adding years to their life, but adding life to their years'. Subsequent chapters will attempt to outline how the therapist can aim to improve not only specific communication skills, but also the quality of life of these patients, despite working outside the traditional clinical setting.

3

Counselling

In Chapter 2 a distinction was made between direct therapy techniques and 'indirect therapy'. Counselling skills are important both in the one to one clinical setting and in less formal work, and speech therapists, like other health and social service workers, have often found themselves in situations where the role of counsellor is forced upon them. Often they do not have the necessary training or support to function effectively as a counsellor. While there are numerous general texts and courses on this subject, it is relevant to consider some of the common problems that can arise within the therapeutic situation.

The British Association for Counselling, in 1980, defined counselling: 'People become engaged in counselling when a person, occupying regularly or temporarily the role of counsellor, offers or agrees explicitly to offer time, attention and respect to another person or persons temporarily in the role of client.'

'The task of counselling is to give the client an opportunity to explore, discover and clarify ways of living more resourcefully and toward greater well-being.'

There are various models which attempt to explain how counselling progresses. Gerard Egan (1981), for example, proposed a three stage model. This describes an initial period of 'exploration and focusing', during which the counsellor establishes the relationship by active listening and responding. Subsequently, understanding of the issues leads to goal setting, as the counsellor offers alternative frameworks, by focusing on the critical themes raised by the client. Finally, action is planned and carried out based on the deeper understanding the client has of his or her own situation. The process aims to encourage the client to work out this 'plan of action' and to evaluate it. It is not for the counsellor to advise on a right course to take.

Thus problems must first be determined and specified as explicitly as possible. In focusing on a problem, it is worth discussing factors that have worsened or helped the situation so far. Either effect may have resulted from attempted solutions. Goals must be specific and realistic (that is, achievable) not only in terms of outcome but in their pacing. Throughout the process the wider family needs to be informed of progress, including professionals and non-related individuals who have a place in the client's current life-style.

It is useful if the therapist/counsellor can take 'time out' to consider the counselling interaction, rather than attempting an objective evaluation when the stresses of that interaction are immediate.

THE COMMUNICATIVELY IMPAIRED CLIENT

Counselling is usually offered and carried out through the medium of the spoken word. Although the counsellor should adjust his language and vocabulary to suit the educational level and the needs of a particular client, in most cases both participants have an adequate level of verbal skill for the process to use this medium.

The speech therapist is, however, by definition working with people who may not have this level of language and speech. Some qualified counsellors are loath to involve themselves with this population, or may not have the knowledge of the nature of the disorder which is necessary, particularly perhaps in terms of the client's ability to understand language.

However, the speech/language impaired will face adjustment problems as will any handicapped individual, and the speech therapist may be the only available person with whom such matters can be raised. It is also true that the one to one therapy setting, within which a relationship of understanding is built up, is often that wherein a client feels most able to discuss any other worries and difficulties he may face.

There are situations when it could be most harmful — both in terms of emotional recovery and adjustment, and in terms of rehabilitating communication skills — to leave a subject unchallenged. The speech therapist, used to a direct advisory and instructing role, may find it difficult initially to assume the role of counsellor. However, she/he may be the professional with the best understanding of the client's problems.

The communication difficulty will mean that the process may well be time consuming. One trap which is important to avoid, is that of stereotyping patients — 'If he is dysphasic, he'll have these adjustment problems'. This approach can certainly speed up the session, but may well miss the client's real concerns! It is important, especially with the speech and language handicapped, to check continually that the exchange is fully understood on both sides. It is also important not to assume causal relationships — a depressed dysarthric patient may not be depressed because of his speech problem, but because of other factors, or indeed may suffer from endogenous depression.

Many factors will affect the client's situation and ability to cope without intervention. These include personal qualities, such as interests, skills, expectations, and values; and also variables related to experience of ill-health and loss in the past, and how these were faced. Situational differences, such as the strength of marital and family relationships, economic constraints, and cultural factors, will also affect how an individual copes.

There must be motivation to engage in the counselling relationship, and readiness to express feelings and discuss what may be highly personal matters. The success of the counsellor in creating an accepting atmosphere will be a large factor in gaining this degree of trust from a client. Confidentiality must be assured.

THE COUNSELLOR

As Rogers (1961) stressed, there is a need for the therapist to recognise first his or her own prejudices, weaknesses and strengths before attempting to help others to achieve greater self-awareness. The therapist/counsellor must be aware what qualities she brings to the interaction, and what her limitations are.

Much has been written of the qualities required by a counsellor. These include the ability to empathise, active listening skills, non-judgemental acceptance of the client (regardless of the nature of the problem), the ability to clarify and organise, flexibility and readiness to respond with warmth, honesty and spontaneity. Many therapists would be taken aback by such a list, but many of these qualities grow as a result of experience within the clinical setting.

There is also the need to be aware of how both verbal and non-verbal communication can convey information. It is crucial that the counsellor transmits congruent verbal and non-verbal messages. Obviously this may be particularly relevant in working with those whose ability to understand verbal information is impaired. Rogers (1961) coined the term 'unconditional positive regard', by which he refers to the need to accept the client without attempting to judge him or the presenting problem. It is very easy to convey a judgemental message non-verbally while verbally assuring the client that he is accepted as a worthy individual.

It is also important that the counsellor feels able to confront the client, in a non-aggressive way. Such confrontation may stem from incongruous messages from the client, or contradictory statements within the counselling session. Obviously confrontation must be used carefully to clarify the client's situation and feelings, not to 'catch him out'. There is also danger of being drawn into an argument with the client. At times it may be best to accept a difference of opinion and progress from that basis. There is a great deal of truth in the words of Herr and Weakland (1979) who state that skilled counsellors 'are differentiated from well-intentioned lay persons largely by what counsellors do *not* do'.

The skill of listening — an active rather than a passive process — is not easily acquired. It demands full attention while the counsellor thinks ahead to other areas to cover or how best to respond. It may be useful to interpret words into their underlying feelings, but only if the client is asked to confirm or deny that interpretation. This will again take more time with a communicatively impaired patient. Non-verbal clues can be useful if, for example, a dysarthric patient conveys verbally that he is not frustrated by his speech difficulty, but demonstrates anger in his tone of voice and gestures when his words are not fully understood.

The counsellor must also be aware of the effect of his or her responses within the interaction. The aims to develop the client's ability to assume responsibility for his own life and to work out his own alternatives and solutions. Thus, open-ended statements and questions will be more helpful than closed questions (which demand only a yes/no response or give a forced alternative option in answering), but may not be possible, for example, when working with aphasic clients. Empathic remarks will often help to reassure the client, both that he is accepted and respected, and that the counsellor is listening. Reflecting back the client's statements can clarify the intended meaning, or reveal contradictions.

Silence also is a form of response, and the counsellor needs to use this rather than to feel that he must fill the gaps, or reassure too quickly. Unrealistic reassurances, even if from the best motives, can handicap the successful progression of the counselling process.

There are dangers in assuming that the client's aims are in line with the therapist/counsellor's. What can be achieved — perhaps more with elderly people than any other section of the population — will depend on the client's perceptions and motivations. Over-involvement is also a common trap into which a counsellor, especially if inexperienced, can fall.

It is, furthermore, most important that the therapist/counsellor recognises that his or her own needs must be met, and that there is the opportunity to obtain support. It may be that the client's difficulties are particularly complicated or upsetting, or that those difficulties raise personal fears or emotions in the counsellor which must then be dealt with.

COUNSELLING WITHIN THERAPY

The communicatively impaired individual faces both a loss and a change in behaviour (Davis and Baggs, 1984). In order to cope he needs the cognitive resources to appraise and adapt to the new situation. The therapist can clarify the situation by sensitive explanations and an outline of the alternative courses of action. She will often need to discover and respond to unrealistic expectations and negative attitudes.

Brumfitt (1985) points out that there are two 'themes' within the therapeutic relationship — the remediation procedure and the underlying feelings about the disorder and its sequelae. She goes on to say 'the situation may break down because of the lack of attention to feelings rather than incorrect remedial manoeuvres'. This becomes crucially important when the stage is reached when speech and language ability has plateaued, and the question of discharge is raised. Too often discharge occurs without attention being given to whether the patient has adjusted to his level of residual impairment and, indeed, whether the family is able to cope. Figure 3.1 illustrates the changing emphasis of therapy, from speech and language restoration to coping with the residual handicap. The latter becomes the emphasis once the person has reached a plateau in terms of communicative recovery. Thus the quality of language *and* the quality of life must be considered.

Figure 3.1: Emphasis of therapy. Based on Wertz (1983)

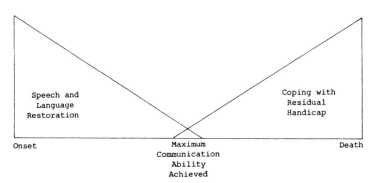

The speech therapist, with her understanding of the nature of the individual's communication disorder, is in the best position to listen to the patient's underlying feelings, without 'jumping' in to speak (or guess) for him.

Impairment in communication reduces the ability to control social functioning, already reduced by the effects of aging, and reduces the ability to effect emotional release. It may be that this release is only possible in the speech therapy clinic, where there tends to be a longer session allocated than in contact with many other health professionals. Denying a patient this opportunity may create additional disorders which will require later management.

Obviously there are those who cope with the adjustment process without the need for specific intervention. Speech therapists, like other professionals, need to find a way to determine which patients and families need counselling, and the extent of intervention. This is unlikely to relate directly either to the specific diagnosis or to the objective severity of the disorder. It will relate to the way in which patients have reacted to earlier losses, and thus gained experience in certain coping behaviours. There will probably also be an element of cultural conditioning in reaction to loss.

If the therapist does not feel able to engage in the counselling process, but feels that such a relationship may help her patient, referral must be considered. The ability to know when to call on more skilled help is one of the skills of a therapist, not a failure.

TYPE OF INTERVENTION

Group therapy

Most of this chapter has focused on the one to one counselling situation, which is the usual setting in which a speech therapist will find herself in the 'counsellor's chair'. There are, however, also group approaches which aim to facilitate psychological adjustment to the handicap, and thus to enhance feelings of self-worth, within a 'social' setting. The communicatively impaired individual faces a changed social milieu, and this will demand new ways of coping with social relationships. The group setting means that role models are available in progressing toward acceptance of their disabilities.

Although there are no formal evaluation studies of such groups for communicatively impaired populations, Oradei and Waite (1974) describe this approach in working with aphasic patients in the United States. Their aim was to allow expression of the feelings aroused by the disability, such as anger, resentment and frustration. This may be most useful when the client/patient has reached a plateau in terms of speech and language recovery, and yet still has not come to terms with the permanent residual deficits.

Speech therapists may gain valuable support and advice by involving other disciplines in organising and running such groups — psychologists, social workers and psychiatric nursing staff, for example, may be interested to participate. If the group includes cultural and racially diverse members it may be most important to obtain the support of those member's families as well. Support groups aimed specifically at relations and friends will be discussed more fully in Chapter 9. Groups may, of course, involve only patients or relatives, or provide a forum for both to meet with other such families.

Family therapy

Formal family therapy has grown from its origins in work with children and with schizophrenics, over the past 30 years, to assume an important role in many areas of psychiatry.

Speech therapists are not trained in family therapy techniques and should refer patients to qualified counsellors. However, the speech therapist may be in the best position to perceive a need, and to be available to a family facing difficulty in adjusting to a handicapped member. Herr and Weakland (1979) quote an example of a speech therapist forced to consider the whole family situation, in working with an aged patient, and this is by no means an uncommon situation.

There are risks to the stability of a family forced to cope with a communicatively impaired member. Haspiel, Clement and Haspiel (1972) comment on the risk of this person becoming a scapegoat for the family's problems. There may also be rejection, overprotection, and role reversals, which need professional intervention in order for the family to recover homeostasis. The therapist's ability to use the 'family language' is important. Failure to avoid professional jargon will result in failure of the family to comprehend the nature of the problem, or to achieve the level of understanding necessary for the counselling process to make progress.

ADJUSTING TO AGING

Having discussed the role of the speech therapist in counselling the communicatively impaired older person, it is important to consider in more detail the underlying needs of elderly people. Merely treating the symptom — be it dysarthria, dyspraxia, aphasia — is not enough, but it is also 'not enough' to attempt to consider the psychological reaction caused by loss of communication skills, outside the context of the individual's general adjustment to their life situation. If there are other, possibly more deep-seated difficulties the speech therapist will often be most likely to be in a position to offer support. There is a need, then, to be aware of the enormity of the adjustments that may need to be made by individuals as they age.

At each stage in life there are certain events and changes, some of which all, and some of which a proportion of people, must face. These carry the potential for positive or for negative coping behaviours and learning experiences. Major transitions (such as marriage, divorce or widowhood) entail passing through a period of uncertainty, between two stable states. If negative learning patterns are established in coping with transitions in youth and middle age, it is likely that there will be difficulties in coping and adjusting to changes later in life. Those who when younger learn positive coping strategies will be more likely to come to an acceptance of age. Erickson described this acceptance in terms of the need 'to be through having been' and 'to face not being'.

Old age leads to a number of enforced changes, the acceptance of which may create psychological difficulties. These changes may include reduced strength, poor health, lack of employment, the loss of family and friends, relocation into a sheltered environment or institution, and the underlying thread which is a loss of independence. Such changes may be perceived as losses, and any one working with elderly people needs to be aware of their need to be allowed to express grief at such events. Bereavement counselling, as a formal process, may be needed by some to enable them to adjust to the loss of health or of home, as well as the more recognised need in coping with the loss of a spouse or child. The aim of counselling is not necessarily to come to welcome a loss, but to accept the fact of it.

Various researchers and theorists have attempted to describe the psychological stages of response to bereavement. Among them is Kubler-Ross who outlined five stages (1974) — shock and denial ('No, not me!') leading on to anger ('Why me?'), preparatory depression ('Woe is me!') and finally to a bargaining attempt ('Yes me, but — ') and acceptance. Not all will achieve that final acceptance, and Kubler-Ross stresses the need for outward looking and opportunity to talk to others in order for 'healing' to occur. In some cases once acceptance is reached it may even be possible to perceive some good in the new situation — as in the person forced to move into a long-term residential home, who eventually can be glad to have the worries of looking after a house taken from them.

The speech therapist may well find herself in a special position, because she tends to be in a more private and longer relationship with a patient than are most other health professionals. Apart from the specific counselling role in relation to a speech or language handicap, it is important that the general problems of accepting age can be raised without embarrassment. The ultimate taboo subject frequently brought up by elderly patients is that of their attitude to death and dying, which may take various forms.

'I am ready to die'

There will be few professionals working in the field of medical gerontology who have not met the older patient who feels ready to die. This is not an expression of suicidal thoughts — a very different matter — but a recognition of the fact of having reached a stage when death can be accepted. This may be a response to his situation and his dependent role, or may be a passive acceptance of the 'next step'.

It may be that active rehabilitation is pushed too hard with some older people, and that in doing so, professional 'carers' compromise the right to dignified death. Many attempt to 'jolly along' patients who express a readiness to die, often with false hope and reassurances. Gabell (1981) urges workers to face the realities of aging, and to be prepared to discuss these most deeply felt feelings.

The subject of death is often embarrassing or difficult to talk about because of the younger clinican's attitude, rather than that of the older patient.

'I am going to die'

While the aim of working with those elderly people who want, or are prepared to die, is to help them to accept life, the aim with those who face terminal illness is to help them to accept death.

Speech therapists may well be involved in working with patients who have cancer, motor neurone disease (amylotrophic lateral sclerosis) or other fatal illnesses. Such patients may or may not fall into the 'elderly' population group, but whatever the age, they will need very careful and sensitive handling.

Kubler-Ross (1974) wrote of the qualities that she found important in working with the dying. Personal experience of illness and/or death in close family or friends was a major factor in helping professionals approach this work. Other qualities were the ability to discuss the situation openly (at the patient's pace), and to reassure that the patient would not be deserted, even though there may be no appropriate medical treatment.

There are four periods when skilled counselling intervention, with the patient and/or their family, may be particularly important (Motor Neurone Disease Association, 1984): (1) at diagnosis; (2) at crisis points throughout the disease (which may be precipitated by changes within the family such as giving up work or going into care); (3) during the terminal stage; and (4) at bereavement. The family will often find it hard to sustain a relationship with an altered spouse or parent, and to accept the role changes necessitated by the progression of the disease. The speech therapist may be involved throughout the course of the illness if, for example, an early sign is any change in speech, voice or language. She may, in some cases, be called later in the course of the disease in order to maintain communication skills or provide an alternative method of communicating.

The patient will often not have a stable attitude towards his condition from diagnosis to death. He may move from aggression to determination to passive acceptance, for example. Denial may occur, and it may be that partial denial is healthy and necessary. The speech therapist needs to be aware of what the patient has been told, and to contribute to team meetings as to how continuing support is organised. The speech therapist should counsel the patient specifically in relation to his communication impairment, but it must be a team decision as to whether this role is extended to a more general counselling function.

COUNSELLING AND THE TEAM APPROACH

The speech therapist's role within the management team will be considered in greater depth in Chapter 8. However, there are some specific points that should be raised in relation to counselling.

There will be patients with whom the speech therapist is involved who require more skilled counselling help than the speech therapist's training and time can handle. There may also be clients with whom a particular clinician finds it hard to cope; occasionally, for example, the nature of the problem may mean the therapist is unable to offer the 'unconditional positive regard' that the counselling relationship necessitates. This is easiest to illustrate in the case of dealing with people who engage in antisocial behaviours, but may also be due to a straightforward personality clash.

If referral to another agency is the course chosen it is important that the client does not feel let down, and supportive contact may be best continued until the referral has been followed up. Reasons for referral should be clearly explained to the client/patient. It can also help to be present at least at the first meeting to explain to the new counsellor the nature of the communication handicap, and how to overcome or adapt to it.

If a team approach is adopted early in the management course, and the need for formal counselling is recognised, it should be a team decision as to who takes on that role. It may be the speech therapist, particularly if there is a severe communication handicap, or another member of the team. Whoever is chosen will face the dilemma of balancing the confidentiality promised within the counselling relationship, against loyalty to 'the team'. Ultimately the extent to which the counsellor reports back to other disciplines involved will be based on his or her personal opinion as to whether that information will enable better management of that patient. The patient should be assured that anything he discusses will be treated as confidential by those concerned in his treatment. It is not usually helpful to promise one to one confidentiality, as there may be important information relating to, or indicating a certain course of, treatment. Furthermore, it can place an enormous burden upon the person in the counselling role, preventing them obtaining support from other team members. Having stressed how important it is for the speech therapist to be aware of the elderly client/patient's emotional and pyschological state, it is worth repeating that the therapist/counsellor will also have needs which must be considered.

4

Communication and Dementia

Psychogeriatrics is the study of psychiatry applied to an elderly population: 'the assessment, treatment and management of elderly people suffering from all kinds of mental disorder' (Pitt 1982). This would include delirium (acute confusion), dementia, depression, mania, paranoid states, neuroses and personality and behaviour disorders.

Speech therapists have, in the past, rarely been involved with this broad category of patients. However, increasingly therapists are being drawn into this field with the recognition that communication is impaired by various mental disorders — most notably dementia and schizophrenia. This chapter will focus on the changing communicative behaviours of dementia patients, and discuss the speech therapist's role with such people.

WHAT IS DEMENTIA?

Dementia, as defined by Pitt (1982), is a 'chronic, progressive brain disease, characterised by intellectual deterioration, impaired memory, and disorientation — all occurring without drowsiness and persisting'.

The recent trend towards study of pragmatic aspects of language, which followed the inclusion of semantics as one of the linguistic sciences, has led some researchers to include language or communicative function impairment in their definitions of dementia (e.g. Bayles, 1984; Bayles et al., 1982).

Dementia is a general diagnosis, which encompasses various conditions that lead to the characteristic memory and intellectual changes (Table 4.1). The most common of these is Alzheimer's disease.

52

Table 4.1: Types of dementia

IRREVERSIBLE
Alzheimer's disease
Multi-infarct
Pick's disease
Subcortical (e.g. Parkinson's disease)
Transmissable (e.g. Jakob-Creutzfeldt Disease)

REMEDIAL
Toxic disorders
Infection
Metabolic disorders
Nutritional defects (e.g. Korsakoff's)
Benign intracranial tumour
Subdural haematoma
Normal pressure hydrocephalus
(sensory deprivation)
(depression)

Alzheimer's disease

Alzheimer's disease (AD) is named after the German neurologist, Alois Alzheimer, who in 1906 described the characteristics of the condition, which had its onset in the presenium. Subsequently the disease which he described and the so-called 'Senile Brain Disease' were recognised as differing only in age of onset. They were categorised as the same disorder in the 1980 Diagnostic and Statistical Manual III. It is said that AD accounts for approximately half of all dementia cases (Bayles, Tomoeda and Caffrey, 1982), but such figures are difficult to collate as diagnosis is by elimination of other causes. The only sure way of diagnosing AD is on autopsy, when characteristic morphological changes are found within the brain.

Neuritic (or senile) plaques are found in the deep cortex and hippocampus. Neuro-fibrillary tangles (which are twisted intra-neuronal fibres woven helically in pairs) and granulovascular degeneration (fluid-filled vacuoles within the cell, surrounded by granular debris) further aid identification of this disease. The process of cell loss is accelerated (Blessed, Tomlinson and Roth, 1968).

Neurochemically there appear to be deficiencies in the cholinergic system, and alterations in noradrenergic neurones. Excessive accumulation of aluminium has also been described (Crapper, Krishnan and Quittkat, 1976).

Research into AD has spiralled over recent years, largely as a result of the increasing numbers of elderly people, and the finding that approximately one in five over-80 year olds will suffer from dementia in one form or another. However, the cause of Alzheimer's disease remains a mystery, despite increasingly optimistic noises from various avenues of research.

Multi-infarct dementia

Multi-infarct dementia, or MID, is the second most common form, accounting for 14 to 20 per cent of all cases of dementia, and another 16 to 20 per cent when there are thought to be two disease processes occurring, i.e. MID alongside Alzheimer's disease (Tomlinson, 1977). Multi-infarct refers to the incidence of numerous transient ischaemic attacks or minor cerebro-vascular accidents, each one causing slightly more residual handicap than the last. Thus the progression of the disease is step-like, rather than the gradual deterioration characteristic of other forms of dementia. Symptoms depend on the location of the infarcts, which seem more likely to occur in the carotid and vertebrobasilar systems (Bayles *et al.*, 1982).

Pick's disease

Pick's disease was described by Arnold Pick in 1892, and resembles Alzheimer's disease. It tends to onset between 40 and 60 years of age, and to be familial. There is characteristic wasting of the frontal and temporal lobes, which can give the appearance of 'horns' on a CT scan.

Although diagnosis is made in the presenium, as with pre-senile Alzheimer's victims, patients tend to be seen eventually by the psychogeriatric team. There is a need for more appropriate provision of care for younger dementia patients, who are often improperly placed in long-stay psychogeriatric units.

Subcortical dementia

The subcortical structures include the deep white matter, the basal ganglia, mammillary bodies, fornix, amygdala and the brainstem (Figures 4.1 and 4.2). Various diseases which affect these structures in some way appear to involve mental changes.

Figure 4.1: The brain stem

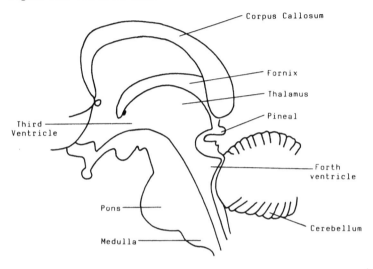

Figure 4.2: The brain — subcortical structures

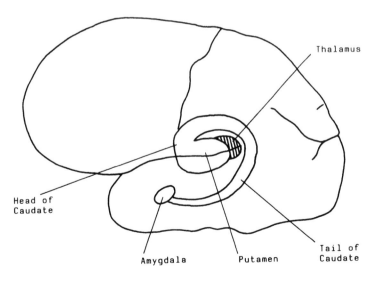

These have been described, for example, in Parkinson's disease, Huntington's chorea, and progressive supranuclear palsy.

The reported incidence of dementia in Parkinson's disease has been variously set between 20 per cent (Pollock and Hornabrook, 1966) and 93 per cent (Pirozzolo *et al.*, 1982). However, it is not known if dementia can be considered a primary symptom in parkinsonism, or if it is due to coexisting Alzheimer's disease in the cortex, or if it is a result of drug therapy.

Huntington's chorea is a primary degenerative dementia. It is an inherited condition resulting in difficulty inhibiting movement, and only surfaces in middle age often after the sufferer has passed on the condition to his or her children. No cure is known and genetic counselling is an important part of management.

Albert (1978) stimulated discussion of the concept of subcortical dementia, and discussed behavioural differences between it and cortical dementia. However, pure subcortical disease appears to be rare.

Korsakoff's disease

Korsakoff's syndrome is the result of nutritional deficiency, usually of vitamin B, as a result of chronic alcoholism. A secondary dementia is characterised by an amnesia for recent events, confabulation and inattention (Bayles *et al.*, 1982).

Transmissable forms

There are transmissable forms of dementia, although they are extremely rare. Kuru is one such form, which is due to a slow-acting virus, and which was prevalent in the cannibalistic Fore tribe of New Guinea. Members of the tribe were infected with the virus by eating diseased brain tissue.

Jakob-Creutzfeldt disease is also viral in nature, and is rapidly progressive, usually leading to death of the infected individual within eighteen months of diagnosis. Any suspicion of this condition means that few pathologists will risk autopsy, as it can be transmitted via contact with the CNS.

Reversible forms

There are causes of dementia in old age which may be treatable. These include syphilis, cerebral tumour, hydrocephalus, and toxic or nutritional deficiency states.

CHARACTERISTIC SIGNS

It is important to remember that many of the symptoms of dementia can be mimicked by other conditions. Confusion of acute onset will share many of the signs, and depression can, not uncommonly, present with similar symptoms. This latter event is described as 'pseudo-dementia'.

The essential features of dementia are intellectual deterioration and impaired memory, especially for recent events. Dyspraxia is typical, and individuals may be emotionally labile. Some are apathetic, others may be aggressive. There may be a paranoid phase, with hallucinations. Other management problems are wandering and incontinence. Attention span decreases, and gradually insight is reduced, although there is often a period of insight early in the course of the disease which is extremely distressing for both sufferer and family. There is also an inherent communication impairment.

While there may be a limited role for one to one speech therapy in the earliest phase of the illness, later many of the characteristic signs of dementia will create the barriers to direct intervention outlined in Chapter 2 — these include lack of insight, memory impairment and inattention, for example.

However, the fact that traditional speech therapy has a minor role does not reduce the importance of recognising the impact that all the dementing diseases have on communication. The effects are discussed below and are summarised in Table 4.2 (p. 62).

THE EFFECTS OF DEMENTIA ON COMMUNICATION

The effect of dementia on communication will be discussed in terms of phonology, vocabulary, grammar and content. It will be apparent that there is a pattern of impairment, with more disruption of semantic and pragmatic aspects of language than of phonology and syntax. This seems to be true in cortical dementia, and in the more controversial subcortical forms; although in the latter language symptoms seem to be more subtle.

Sub cortical lesions will also, however, cause dysarthric symptoms characterised by monotony, syllabic stressing and fading volume. If there is an accompanying dementia then the speech therapist must decide whether formal intervention aiming to offer therapy for the dysarthric symptoms is appropriate. Provision of alternative communication systems or aids may also be affected by any intellectual deterioration.

Phonology

Phonology remains unaffected through the early and middle stages in most cases. In the late stage errors are not uncommon, but this aspect of communication remains the most well preserved. This generally accepted fact is borne out by several studies, including that of Whitaker (1976) who made a case study of an echolalic dement, who in repetition tasks corrected phonological errors (and syntactic errors) made deliberately by the examiner.

The exception to this may be the multi-infarct dementia subject, where the location of infarcts may lead to difficulties in phonological aspects of language, which are dysphasic in nature.

Vocabulary

Early stage. There may be signs, even in the earliest phase, that the individual's vocabulary is reduced. This may be indicated at first by slight word-finding difficulty, which many patients and relatives attribute to the aging process.

Middle stage. The patient presents gradually with a more and more marked reduction in vocabulary, and increasingly relies on automatic and social speech. Naming is affected, with an apparent loss of semantic distinctions and thus overgeneralisation of terms. Schwartz, Marin and Saffran (1979) describe this as a 'progressive breakdown in referential specificity', and feel that lexical processes may be more vulnerable to the effects of diffuse cerebral pathology than the more 'tightly wired' syntactic and phonological processes.

The naming deficit in dementia has stimulated some interesting discussion as to its underlying nature. Rochford's (1971) much quoted study attributed this naming difficulty to visual misperception, and described his dementing subjects as 'verbally fluent but perceptually off-course'. Kirschner, Webb and Kelly (1982) contradicted this view, reporting that increased naming errors occurred with increased abstraction of stimuli, for both Alzheimer's and normal subjects. Bayles and Tomoeda (1983) found that errors were both more common and more likely to be unrelated to the stimulus, the more severe the level of dementia. They felt that there was no evidence of visual difficulties outside the work on language, but that the breakdown was at the stage of matching the incoming visual signal to its lexical reference — 'a linguistic-cognitive defect'. The debate continues, with at least the possibility of some perceptual deficit contributing to naming difficulties.

Word association tasks, such as those used by Gewirth, Schindler and Hier (1984), have demonstrated an increase in the number of idiosyncratic and null responses as the disease progresses. Gewirth and his colleagues argue that this represents a loss of semantic markers, while syntactic-lexical knowledge is better preserved. This is further supported by the unchanged proportion of syntagmatic responses, but proportionate decrease in paradigmatic associations.

Late stage. At the end of the disease course there is marked anomia, grossly reduced vocabulary, increasing impairment of word comprehension, and gradually increasing use of neologisms, paraphasic errors and jargon.

Grammar

Early stage. The early stage of the disease is not characterised by syntactic and morphological errors.

Middle stage. While syntax is relatively well preserved there may be increased use of sentence fragments and deviations. This seems to stem not from syntactic breakdown, but from word finding and/or attentional deficits — a view which is not yet backed up by empirical study. Bayles and Tomoeda's (1984) study of written discourse did not find a difference in the use of grammatical sentences between dementia patients and normal subjects. Their dementing subjects did show, however, a decrease in organisation, relevance and the number of words used.

Late stage. Comprehension of grammatically complex structures is poor, both of the spoken and written word. Expression, in the final stages, is marked by use of incomplete syntactic structures.

Content

Early stage. Bayles (1986) writes: 'the less dependent the rules of a system are on conscious awareness for their application, the less vulnerable the system is to the effects of dementia'. When looking at the content of language, and the way in which an individual uses language, it is a conscious process which is being considered.

The patient may drift from the topic, and demonstrates difficulty in generating a series of relevant utterances. His output is thus vague and rambling, although he retains the 'social skill' of knowing when to take his turn in conversation. Initiation of conversation may not be appropriate.

New information and 'difficult' linguistic structures, such as analogy, sarcasm and non-literal statements, are not understood and assimilated. However, at this stage there may be elements of insight, and many use 'cover up strategies'. de Ajuriaguerra and Tissot (1975) found that patients with 'senile dementia' employed confabulation, indignation, anxiety and admission of difficulty as coping strategies when faced with problematic tasks.

Middle stage. As the disorder progresses there is increasing difficulty sticking to the topic, and fewer ideas are expressed. Perseveration is common, as in many brain-injured patients. Bayles and her colleagues (1985), who wisely are attempting to subgroup dementia subjects by aetiology, found a decrease in the number of ideas as the severity increased.

The awareness of when to talk seems to be retained; but the patient's sensitivity to his conversational partner is markedly less acute. At this stage few patients are able to take into account such factors as shared knowledge, topic relevance and time scale. There is less adherence to the 'conversational maxims' that govern normal conversation (Bayles, 1984). de Ajuriaguerra and Tissot (1975) describe the expressive language of the dementia victim as serving 'as an auxiliary to action, but not as a vehicle for explicit thought'.

Pragmatic processing involves perception, attention and abstraction among other cognitive functions, and therefore it may be expected that it is an area rapidly affected by the dementing process. Too little attention has been paid to this in studies undertaken so far, although in terms of language use it has been noted that perlocutionary acts decrease (that is, utterances that have an effect on the listener) and illocutionary acts (that is, acts performed by the utterance) become less diverse. Shekum and LaPointe (1984) looked at discourse in Alzheimer's disease, and found more exophoric reference, sentence deviations and long pauses; and fewer cohesive ties.

Late stage. As dementia worsens there is a decrease in attempts to cover up or correct errors, due presumably to lack of insight. The ability to produce a sequence of related ideas is lost, and the content is often bizarre and irrelevant. This may reflect the increased egocentricity of language and thought, upon which numerous researchers have commented. Talk of the past, in relation to victims' own lives, is most lucid. Perseveration of ideas worsens, and there is also marked repetition of words and phrases.

Generally the individual is, by this stage, unaware of surroundings and context. Some withdraw from communication, which Stevens (1985) suggests may be a feature of end-stage dementia. Others may enter a stage of echolalia, or of palilalia, or produce bizarre jargon strings. Variations in language symptoms probably reflect the distribution of neural lesions and cell loss.

Having broadly outlined characteristic alterations in communication in dementia, it is important that they are recognised as generalisations. Dementia involves piecemeal changes in the neural tissue, and specific symptoms will vary depending on the sites involved in any one individual. This is especially relevant

Table 4.2: Dementia and communication

	Mild	Moderate	Severe
General	STM deficit Disorientation Change of affect Avoidance strategies	Increased STM/LTM deficits Poor concentration Ideational perseveration Apathy Inability to manage personal affairs Lack of correction of errors Lack of insight	Increased disorientation and memory loss Repetitive movements Inappropriate social behaviour Poor eye contact Wandering
Language sounds	Used correctly	Used correctly	Generally correct, but errors not uncommon
Words	Vocabulary reduced May complain of word-finding difficulty	Anomia in conversation and on testing Relies on auto-matisms Noticeably reduced vocabulary May use semantic paraphasias	Lack of word comprehension May use jargon/neologisms Marked anomia
Grammar	Generally correct	Sentence fragments and deviations Grammatically complex sentences may not be fully understood Inadequate use of functors Ellipsis	Lack of compre-hension of many grammatical forms Further syntactic breakdown
Content	May drift from topic Vagueness Reduced ability to generate series of relevant sentences Personalised/egocentric language	Repetition of ideas 'Losing' topic Fewer ideas expressed Talks about past events	Unable to produce a sequence of related ideas Often irrelevant and bizarre Echolalia 'Empty' speech
Use	Long winded but knows when to respond Failure to initiate conversation when appropriate Difficulty following humour, analogy, sarcasm, etc.	Recognises questions Loss of sensitivity to conversational partners Rarely corrects errors Lack of communi-cative intent	Unaware of context Insensitive to partners Little relevant language May be mute or jargoning

in multi-infarct dementia, where specific disabilities, such as aphasia or dyspraxia, may co-occur with the effects on communication of diffuse cerebral damage. Other compounding variables will include the incidence of depression, and other pathological conditions.

In summary, it may be said that pragmatic and semantic aspects are those affected earliest and to the greatest degree in dementia, while phonology and grammar are better preserved. However, to the forefront of the clinicians's mind must be the awareness that patients diagnosed as suffering from dementia do not form an homogenous group.

DIFFERENTIAL DIAGNOSIS

Dementia and normal aging

Language and cognition are inextricably linked, and neither can be fully assessed in isolation from the other. There are changes in both which occur as a result of normal (that is, non-pathological) aging. In order, therefore, to assess whether a person is showing normal developmental patterns or may be in the early stages of dementia, detailed baseline norms are necessary. It is rarely difficult to distinguish an individual if the dementia is moderately or severely advanced, when behavioural observations alongside a case history can often provide the necessary information. However, it is not uncommon to be faced with a differential diagnostic dilemma if the individual might be mildly demented. The question is not academic, as a misplaced label will have critical effects on how that person is treated both by family and professionals.

There is an increasing body of evidence that certain language tasks may be particularly sensitive in indicating minimal dementia. Bayles and Boone (1982) looked at commonly used psychological tests, including the Block Design subsection of the Wechsler Adult Intelligence Scale (WAIS), and the Nonsense Syllable Learning Test (NSLT). These they compared with five language tasks 'selected because of their putative dependence on cognitive processes'. These tasks were story retelling, sentence correction (of semantic, syntactic and phonological errors), sentence disambiguation, verbal expression (via an object description task), and naming. Statistical analysis found that the most sensitive tasks, to separate mildly affected dements from normal controls were in fact those language measures that involved semantic judgement, and the verbal expression task. Among the five most weighted variables, only the Mental Status Questionnaire (Goldfarb, 1975) was found of the psychological measures investigated.

If these results can be replicated, and extended to consider other language measures there could be far-reaching implications for the role of the speech therapist in the management team. It could encourage involvement at the initial assessment, and in the diagnosis of dementia, and would suggest that a language-based screening text would have a useful role to play.

Dementia versus aphasia

The most frequent differential diagnosis that the speech therapist is called upon to make in this field is that between dementia and aphasia.

The Diagnostic and Statistical Manual III viewed aphasia as a 'possible associate of dementia', and even now this view is

Table 4.3: Dysphasia/dementia: differential diagnostic features

	Dementia	Dysphasia
Onset	Insidious, progressive deterioration	Acute with some improvement and plateau of residual impairment
Mood and behaviour	Inconsistent behaviour Labile, shallow affect Becomes oblivious to surroundings Rarely initiates activity Inappropriate social behaviour	Consistent behaviour Mood varies Often frustration Initiates activity Usually appropriate social behaviour
Memory	Marked deficits, especially of recent memory Unable to retain information and learn Immediate recall better than delayed	Generally intact Learning ability largely intact Immediate recall may be as limited as delayed
Cognition	Generalised impairment and disorientation Lack of insight	Generally intact, but verbal intelligence measures will be affected Insight varies (usually poorer with low comprehension)

Table 4.3: Dysphasia/dementia: differential diagnostic features *(continued)*

	Dementia	Dysphasia
Perceptual and sensory loss	Difficult to manage/compensate for sensory deficits Perceptual difficulties	Sensory deficits can be compensated for May be perceptual problems, in *addition* to dysphasic symptoms
Fluency	– – – – May be fluent or non fluent – – – –	
Pragmatics	Egocentric Eventual failure to conform to conversational rules and context Poor eye contact Lack of desire to communicate Has conversational sensitivity	Often socially appropriate within limitations of language disorder Retains conversational sensitivity
Verbal repetition	Often intact, but may be echolalic with no understanding	Impaired
Gesture	Rarely uses gesture May be distracted by use of gesture by others	May use gesture Often comprehension helped if others use gestures
Articulation	Preserved until later stages	Preserved
Phonology	Preserved until later stages	Often impared with paraphasic errors
Syntax	Reduced complexity but largely intact until late stages	Disordered (paragrammatic/telegrammatic/agrammatic)
Semantics	Reduced vocabulary and semantic paraphasic errors Jargon may develop	Restricted vocabulary and paraphasic errors
Organisation and relevance	Increasing vagueness and irrelevance Ideational perseveration	May be largely appropriate within limits of language difficulties; or may be circumlocutive and irrelevant (especially Wernicke's)
Therapy/stimuli	Tends not to respond to cueing Great effect of manner/type of presentation Distractible	Often helped by phonological or semantic cues

Source: Based on Bayles *et al.* (1982) and Stevens (personal communication)

widely held among medical and other health workers. However, the communicative impairment in dementia should not just be considered in terms of language breakdown, but should be viewed as a total. The use of the specific term 'aphasia' carries misleading connotations.

It is confusing to talk of diagnosing dementia and aphasia, when describing the language impairment of the former as being the latter. There are also connotations carried by the term 'aphasia', of acute onset, a degree of recovery, and subsequent stabilisation, none of which would apply to the communication disorder in dementia. The term currently preferred is the 'language of dementia', which does at least make this valid and important semantic distinction. This is not to imply that the two conditions cannot occur side by side — indeed it is not uncommon to find the patient with multi-infarct dementia who has aphasia, as a result of a focal lesion; and any dementia victim is, of course, still open to the risk of CVA or other brain trauma.

Often differential diagnosis can be made as a result of behavioural observations and a full case history. However, there are those cases which present a more difficult diagnostic problem.

Table 4.3 outlines some of the commonly used differential points between dementia and dysphasia. It may be apparent that while generalisations are made, they frequently base on a moderate or severe dementia patient. For example, it may be reasonable to say that the severe dementia victim has no insight, but some retain a degree of insight in the early stages (which is usually when differential diagnosis is difficult). Similarly, the aphasia patient who fits the moderate-severe Wernicke's sub-category may well present with no insight. The aphasic may in the acute stages be disorientated, and self care and continence may well be affected by the somatic sequelae of a CVA. Thus no strict rules can be made on which to base a decision as important as this. There is even no clear case in assessing cognitive functioning, partly because of the imprecise way in which pre-morbid intelligence is assumed, and also because of the difficulty in finding tasks that do not include language at some point in their presentation, reasoning or response.

The most difficult distinction is often seen as between the dementing person and the Wernicke's (fluent; aphasic. Obler *et al.* (1985) found, in fact, that Alzheimer's subjects of mild-moderate severity were more likely anomic than Wernicke's asphasics. Their dementing group was more informative and used fewer neologisms and paraphasic errors than did the Wernicke's. However, the severity of aphasic impairment and of the level of dementia, does affect these parameters.

Bayles *et al.* (1985) point out that there are shared features between dementia and aphasia, but stress the fact that differences are apparent in the underlying cause and in the quality of error. Perseveration, for example, is found in patients suffering from both conditions — in dementia, however, it tends to be a perseveration of ideas and themes, and in aphasia, of linguistic units. Similarly, circumlocution in dementia is thought to stem from forgotten linguistic intention, but in aphasia to be the result of word-finding difficulties.

The next section of this chapter will discuss assessment, but it is worth being aware, while considering differential diagnosis, of a series of case studies in the literature (e.g. Mesulam, 1982; Cole, Wright and Banker, 1979). These describe a language disturbance of a progressive nature, which they term 'slowly progressive aphasia', without signs of generalised dementia for many years — in some cases up to eleven years post-onset. It appears that there may be a selective degeneration of the left perisylvian fissure, and that the condition may bear some relation to Pick's disease. While such cases are rare, they may appear in the speech therapy clinic, and that discipline would be central in their management.

ASSESSMENT

The speech therapist who attempts to separate language assessment from cognition will gain little useful information. Assessment will need a multidisciplinary base.

The case history

The first step, whenever it is possible, is to take a complete history, involving relatives and friends of the individual to be assessed. The assessment format in the appendix (p. 73) includes many of the relevant areas to cover, and it is likely that the speech therapist will see the patient after other team members have obtained this information.

Information about the individual's communication problem will be useful, alongside other behavioural changes. The speech therapist should ask about the onset of the communication difficulty, whether it was acute or gradual, what the initial problem was, and how this has developed. The relative's views on their communicative relationship will be important. Insight into the difficulty should also be assessed. Carers attending hospital are likely to find that they are continuously asked the same questions, and a brief explanation as to their relevance may well ease their frustration.

While taking a history it is useful to gather as much information as possible about the individual's past life and interests. The opportunity to increase knowledge about the patient needs to be taken, as carers cannot always be involved in subsequent visits. Such questions can provide useful information towards planning future management, and maximising the person's desire to communicate.

Medical history

As much information as necessary should be gathered from the medical notes, and from other disciplines. Certain investigations, to eliminate reversible causes, will or should have been carried out. Others may reveal information about the extent of brain damage, and location of lesions (e.g. CT scans, regional blood flow charts, pneumoencephalography and electro-encephalography). It is important to discover the patient's prescribed medication, as various drugs do affect communication. Some of those prescribed in psychiatric disorders are included in Table 2.4 (p. 33).

Communication

It has already been commented that the separation of language and thought is of little clinical value. Any test battery must include measures of both cognition and language if it aims fully to assess the patient suspected of suffering from dementia. Bayles *et al.* (1982) feel that a battery should include measures of the following skills and functions: learning, recent and remote memory, associative thought, orientation, ability to abstract, visuospatial reasoning, expressive and receptive language, verbal fluency and verbal reasoning. Such a list will necessitate a multidisciplinary approach.

If all those aspects should be assessed, the question remains as to how, for within the field of language and communication there are no standardised assessments for use with a dementing population. This has led to the use of language batteries such as the Boston Diagnostic Aphasia Examination (Goodglass and Kaplan, 1983). Wertz (1984) makes the point that if one finds a deficit using an aphasia test, it is likely that it will be assumed to reflect an aphasic impairment. He argues that such tests are of little or no value in the case of the dementing patient. Despite this, many clinicians have lifted sub-tests from language batteries, and used them as a basis for their own assessments. There remains the need for a standard, structured assessment of the communicative behaviours of dementia. This should be weighted towards the semantic and pragmatic, and be heavily oriented to demonstrating functionally relevant information (either in terms of diagnosis or management).

The most sensitive language tasks are those which are active, non-automatic, generative or dependent on reason.

There are always cases which defy diagnosis, and in such cases, when dementia is suspected, the only solution is to reappraise the situation after a time gap. If dementia is present a deterioration would usually have occurred after a six month delay.

MANAGEMENT

Early stage

If language tasks are proven to be particularly sensitive to early intellectual deterioration (that is, more so than the commonly used neuropsychological tests) the speech therapist may find herself playing an increasingly important role in management, as well as in diagnosis. Screening could be used to allow early detection of reversible forms (and thus lead to appropriate intervention) or of irreversible dementias, when early 'social' intervention can be of great value to carers.

69

Direct one to one speech therapy is often dismissed out of hand when dealing with dementing patients. However, not all therapists would accept this. Bayles (1984) wrote: 'For patients remaining in the mild stages for several years, (individual) therapy may markedly improve their existence and that of their loved ones'. In Great Britain, Walker (1984) expressed a similar view: 'It seems reasonable to suggest that aphasia therapy techniques specific to these (that is, the demented person's) errors may have a place in dementia, particularly where early intellectual failure has been identified'. There has not been any attempt to evaluate the benefit of therapy with such clients, but intuitively it seems reasonable that in the early stage it may benefit some dementia patients. However, it is unlikely that such benefits will last long, and it is not common for early stage dementia patients to reach the speech therapist. The exception is the patient who initially presents with a language disorder, and who should be given a trial period of functionally based therapy whenever possible.

If individual therapy is undertaken, the clinician must be aware of other effects of the disease process in planning methods and materials. Tasks which demand too great an ability in memory or abstract reasoning for example should be substituted or adapted. Materials should take account of possible perceptual deficits, and of sensory deficits which are harder to manage in the confused or demented person. Distractions inherent in multi-stimuli presentation or in using unfamiliar forms of presentation should be avoided. Materials should also reduce the need for interpretation and inference (Stevens, 1985a).

Middle stage

The speech therapist has an important, if indirect, role with dementia victims at this stage, and with their families. One of the first steps should be to identify, objectively, the most effective ways of adapting the carers' communication skills to compensate for the patient's difficulties. In working with the aphasic or dysarthric, for example, it is the patient's skills that the therapist attempts to modify. This being impossible for the moderate-severe dementia victim, any adaptation must be in his communicative partner. The end result — improvement in the communication process — will be the same.

Thus, both professional and lay carers will need full explanations of what communication involves *before* they are asked to adapt their behaviours. If this explanation is neglected, carers will not understand why they are asked to alter certain of their behaviours, and consequently will be less motivated to do so. Most carers are not aware of the variables of communication which lie within their powers to control — variables such as topic, amount of new information, speaking rate, word choice, use of analogy, humour and sarcasm. There may also be environmental variables that can be manipulated to maximise the chances of successful communication.

Involvement with the family will be discussed more fully in a later chapter, but it is an important role for the speech therapist, who can ensure that the carer does not mislabel certain language and speech problems. It may also be appropriate for the therapist to be involved in group therapies, such as Reality Orientation. These will also be discussed in a later chapter.

Late stage

The gradual deterioration that characterises dementia means that advice will need to be constantly updated, and continuing support offered to the carers. It may be that some families will require more professional support than others; and some will find useful support from outside organisations such as the Alzheimer's and Related Disorders Society.

The lack of any cure for the majority of dementing conditions has led to dementia being described as a social, rather than a medical problem. To some extent all professions working with these patients will be, or will have been, forced to rethink their traditional roles. The speech therapist, by the late stage of the disease process, will have a purely advisory or consultative role.

RESEARCH

There has been an increasing amount of research undertaken in the broad field of dementia, and specifically in the field of language. Some of these studies have shaped the present clinical role of the speech therapist, others, if replicated, could influence this role in the future. Among the latter is the work on the sensitivity of language tests (e.g. Bayles and Boone, 1982), which may also mean that such tasks can be used to measure the effects of behavioural and pharmacological intervention.

Much more information is needed on how communication is affected in the different forms of dementia, and at different levels of severity. The tendency to lump together aetiological subgroups may well have corrupted some large group studies, as Bayles points out. Similarly while many would agree with Bayles in feeling that speech therapy does have 'a vital role', it is important that this is looked at more objectively. One approach may be for clinicians to accumulate single case studies, to establish an information bank. However, the methodological problems already seen in attempting to evaluate the efficacy of therapy with aphasic patients are even greater in looking at dementia.

There is an exciting future for speech-language therapists working in this field, with increasing opportunities for research as well as clinical work. It does, however, place a burden on the therapist, who must adapt to working with people who face only deterioration in their condition, and with their families, who must attempt to survive in apparently unbearable situations.

APPENDIX 4:

Areas to cover in initial assessment

1. Physical health
   — general appearance
   — hearing
   — vision
   — sleep pattern
   — continence
   — mobility
   — physical complaints
   — smoking

2. Self care
   — washing
   — dressing
   — eating and diet
   — cooking
   — financial arrangements
   — housing arrangements

3. Cognition and behaviour
   — wandering
   — orientation (person; place; time)
   — language
   — delusions
   — hallucinations
   — mood
   — aggression

4. Present resource systems involved

5. Details of primary carer

5

Sensory Changes, Disorders and Management

The communication chain described in Chapter 1 illustrates the fact that the reception of a message is as crucial for successful communication to occur, as is the sending. This applies whether the message is conveyed through the auditory, the visual, or another medium. Thus the speech therapist must be aware of sensory changes due to the aging process, and how sensory disorders affect communication. Such knowledge will be important in assessment and management of older people with speech or language disorders, but in addition the speech therapist may have a primary role to play in working with, for example, the hearing-impaired older individual.

This chapter, while focusing mainly on hearing and the aging process, will also look at the nature of sensory changes and disorders in general. The impact of visual or tactile impairment, for example, on communication has been sadly neglected both in research and in clinical work.

HEARING

The greatest age-linked barrier to effective communication is the risk of a disabling degree of hearing loss, that is, a level of hearing difficulty that results in a reduced ability to function normally in daily life. Table 5.1 gives prevalence estimates of hearing loss in over 65-year-olds, and although it is important to remember that patterns of distribution are more relevant than incidence figures *per se* (Davis, 1983), it is interesting to note that more than 18 per cent of this age group have better-ear hearing losses of over 55 dB.

74

SENSORY CHANGES, DISORDERS AND MANAGEMENT

Table 5.1: Prevalence estimates of hearing loss in over 65-year-olds. National study of hearing

Hearing level	Prevalence estimates (%)	
	Better ear	Worse ear
> 15	74.8	86.2
> 25	47.9	63.9
> 35	28.0	42.4
> 45	16.7	29.0
> 55	9.4	16.0
> 65	4.6	10.9
> 75	2.6	7.7
> 85	1.5	4.6
> 95	0.4	2.6

Source: MRC Institute of Hearing Research, Nottingham, England, July 1985.

The speech therapist is thus likely to find a high proportion of elderly patients presenting either with a hearing loss that has led to a secondary communication difficulty or that coexists with a primary communication disorder.

Aging and hearing

Figure 5.1: Structure of the human ear

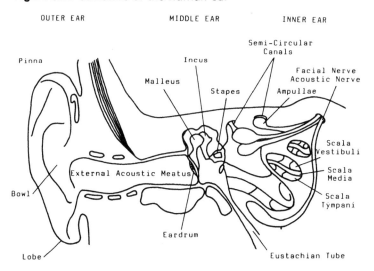

75

Figure 5.1 shows the structure of the human ear. With aging structural changes occur in the pinna, and in the external auditory meatus where tissues thin and become less elastic. The tympanic membrane may thin, or be subject to pathological sclerotic thickening. Within the middle ear the ossicular chain becomes more rigid, and there are typically degenerations and atrophy of the muscles and ligaments of the middle ear (Klotz, 1963). There may be some alterations in function of the eustachian tube (Nerbonne, unpublished).

However, it is changes in the inner ear that are accepted as most influential in causing less acute hearing in older people; sensory neural hearing losses being much more common in that age group than conductive losses. General atrophy of the organ of corti occurs, with hair cell loss and alterations (Gacek, 1975). The basilar membrane appears to show increasing stiffness. The auditory nerve is significantly changed, with the loss of ganglion cells in the spiral ganglia, and narrowing of the internal auditory meatus. Neurones are lost throughout the central nervous system from an early age, and this continues through life and involves those areas which play a role in auditory processing.

Auditory assessment

Initial examination

Audiological assessment should include a full case history and medical examination before specific audiometric measures are taken. The case history should provide information as to the onset and symptoms, including any relevant past medical or social factors. It is also useful to discover why the client has presented in the clinic at that particular time; whether, for example, he has been pushed into attending by his family, or his motivation was a result of his own perception of hearing loss.

Information about the person's drug regime may be helpful. Chermak and Jinks (1981) point this out from a pharmacological viewpoint, indicating the need to be aware that many drugs prescribed for older people can cause ototoxicity (e.g. aminoglycoside, antibiotics and loop diuretics). They stress the need for clear instructions although, as was seen in Table 2.5, there are additional problems in drug dosage and compliance in elderly people.

The medical examination will be the job of the physician, but

SENSORY CHANGES, DISORDERS AND MANAGEMENT

it is important that relevant information is passed on to the other disciplines involved in management. If the hearing loss is causing or compounding a communication difficulty this would naturally include the speech therapist. However, it may be possible to manage a loss purely at the level of provision of an aid.

Pure tone audiometry

Pure tone audiometry requires the patient to respond when a tone is delivered to one ear, via bone and/or air conduction. Individual test tones at specified frequencies are presented at various intensities, and an audiogram (such as that in Figure 5.2) is plotted to show the threshold level for each frequency. If there is a difference between air and bone conduction audiograms it can be diagnostically significant, indicating whether a loss is conductive or sensori-neural.

Figure 5.2: Audiogram of normal hearing

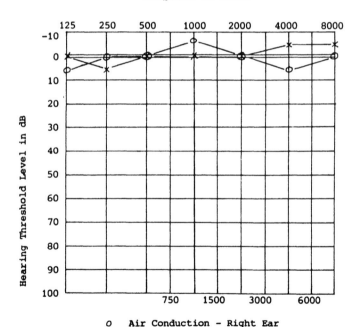

77

Speech audiometry

Pure tone thresholds are useful but do not indicate the ability to hear and to discriminate speech. Some people may only have a minimal loss of auditory sensitivity, but have poor discrimination skills. These are affected by central factors, such as slowed processing and distractibility, and by physical and social variables.

Speech audiometry is made up of several tests. Speech reception threshold (SRT) requires the listener to repeat words, which decrease in intensity until only 50 per cent are correctly repeated. The Speech Discrimination Test involves presentation of phonetically balanced word lists at a 'comfortable' intensity. The percentage of words repeated is then calculated to give the 'discrimination score'. Such tests can be adapted to assess how individuals cope in difficult listening conditions.

Other audiometric tests

The audiometrician may also undertake impedance testing, using tympanometry or acoustic reflex testing, if this is felt to be necessary. There are also special site of lesion batteries, which involve Bekesy testing, alternate binaural loudness balance, and tone decay testing. Electrophysiological testing includes cortical and brain stem evoked responses.

Self assessment

It is essential that the everyday influence of hearing loss is considered. Most testing is carried out in clinical conditions which do not reflect the person's functional ability to cope with a loss of hearing. That is, standard hearing tests may provide a quantitive measure of loss, but do not indicate qualitatively what that loss means to the sufferer. Self-assessment tools, as an adjunct to standard testing, can be used to indicate the effect that a hearing loss has on behaviour and to point out the person's needs in terms of rehabilitation. There are various scales described in the literature (e.g. High, Fairbanks and Glorig, 1964; Ventry and Weinstein, 1982), which tend to consider emotional and social-situational adjustment. Some such scales are designed or adapted for an elderly population, and are discussed by Garstecki (1981). They should include some questions specifically related to communicative experiences and perceptions.

Problems in testing the elderly

Quite apart from any pathological condition affecting hearing, there are other factors which may make audiometric assessment of elderly people difficult.

Structural changes may cause difficulty in presenting the sound; Zucker and Williams (1977) note a high incidence of collapsed canals. There is also the influence of somatic and psychological illness, which can cause problems; for example, it is most difficult to obtain reliable results from individuals who suffer from dementia. Mobility problems mean that many cannot attend a clinic, and must be tested, therefore, in what are often far from ideal conditions. Off-site assessment also limits the nature of the tests that can be administered, and because of the altered environment means that interpretation of results must be carefully considered.

Elderly people have been found to respond over cautiously in all sensory threshold tasks (Botwinick, 1973), and audiometric results will be affected by this factor. Caution, allied with an increased reaction time means that there may be overestimation of hearing loss unless great care is taken. This care should extend from the assessment procedure to the interpretation of results.

Auditory problems common in an elderly population

Presbyacusis

Presbyacusis is sometimes defined as the hearing impairment that occurs as a result of aging; but it is a pathological state, and does not have a one to one relationship with age *per se*. It is characterised by hearing loss which is more marked in the higher frequencies (Figure 5.3).

The early literature attributed this condition to structural changes in the cochlear, but subsequently various subgroups of presbyacusis have been described. Schuknecht and Igarashi (1964), for example, labelled four categories as being sensory, neural, metabolic and mechanical.

The auditory manifestations of presbyacusis are decreased acuity and speech discrimination. The high frequency sounds are not heard, and therefore speech is perceived in a distorted fashion. The precise pattern of auditory impairment will

SENSORY CHANGES, DISORDERS AND MANAGEMENT

Figure 5.3: Hearing loss with aging

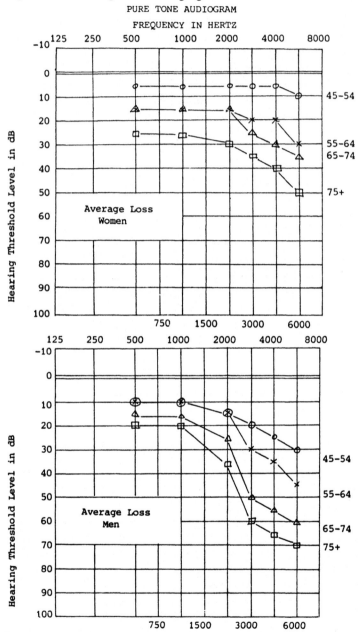

O Air Conduction — Right Ear; X Air Conduction — Left Ear
△ Bone Conduction — Right Ear; □ Bone Conduction — Left Ear

depend on the type, or types, of presbyacusis, which in turn depend on the location of defects within the auditory pathway. Threshold sensitivity drops, and pitch discrimination is less precise. The condition may be revealed by a speech reception threshold raised over and above the pure tone threshold. Stressful listening conditions present greater difficulty. The cognitive processes which 'utilise the input to mediate behavioural responses' (Corso, 1977), play a role in the way in which presbyacusis manifests itself.

Recruitment

Recruitment is prevalent among older people. Functionally it restricts the 'auditory space' by bringing the pain threshold down towards the (often raised) hearing threshold. This, as Bamford (1982) points out is a major obstacle to speech perception, and also to the use of amplification.

Tinnitus

Tinnitus is a noise heard in the ear which does not have an external source; it is a symptom, not a disease (Davis, 1983). Prevalence is a function of age, particularly in the case of severe tinnitus, which is found in approximately three per cent of 61–70-year-olds. It is a not infrequent accompaniment of deafness in elderly people, and creates a disproportionate handicap. Other age-related factors of cerebral function may increase the level of disability even further.

The psychosocial effect of hearing loss

Hearing impairment at any age can have a profound effect on psychological well being. That psychological impact exists even at the stage of diagnosis. Veron, Griffin and Yoken (1981) found that patients waited on average five years before seeking help, which the authors attributed to a denial resulting from fear of being thought to fit the stereotype of being 'old and deaf'. That five year wait is destructive in that the problems in coping are compounded, and adjustment is further delayed.

Hearing difficulty places the sufferer in a strange and unreal environment. He understandably, therefore, feels less secure and more anxious. Emotional disturbances that already exist can be accentuated, as can psychiatric disorders such as paranoia. The degree of social interaction, however, may not be related as directly as was once thought. Norris and Cunningham (1981), bearing in mind their study only considered presbyacusis in otherwise healthy elderly subjects, found increased hearing loss correlated with either increases *or* decreases in amount of social interaction. It may, of course, be that hearing loss affects social life more in quality than quantity of interaction.

Hearing loss, of course, affects not only ability to interact socially by following speech, but also means that environmental sounds (such as traffic, sirens, bells) may not be heard and this can result in considerable disorientation.

The effect of hearing loss on communication

Watts (1983) states that 'The major impact of hearing loss . . . is in the area of communication'. This is true for the hearing-impaired person in the role of the 'sender' as well as 'receiver'. Obviously listening will be affected, and often attempts may be made to 'cover-up', by projecting the blame on to others for 'mumbling' or 'not speaking up', or by filling in conversation with insufficient clues. If a hearing loss develops gradually many individuals will compensate accordingly — by turning up the radio or television volume, making sure they can see the speaker, and so on. The ability to cope is affected by many variables, and differs enormously between individuals.

The hearing loss may well, however, also affect a person's ability as a speaker. Parker (1983) felt that 'a change in the ability to monitor speech auditorily may cause a significant deterioration of speech in a previously normal speaker, and this may considerably worsen the overall communication problem if appropriate and early help is not given'. Parker goes on to outline segmental and suprasegmental changes that may occur in adults who develop a hearing loss. Segmental changes would include phonetic details, such as reduced consonant clusters, insertion of syllables between sounds and words, and possible centralisation of vowel sounds. Suprasegmental aspects which may be affected include: voice — monitoring of loudness, and deletion of the lower end of the pitch range (resulting in a narrower range that may be perceived as a raised pitch level); intonation — partly as a result of the restricted pitch range, and inappropriate attempts to compensate for this by working on loudness stressed; and timing and rhythm. Frequently noted is the possibility of hypernasality, but this may be due to an exaggeration of a normal coarticulation effect on words which include nasal consonants (Binnie, Danilof and Buckingham, 1982) and does not seem to occur often in elderly people who develop a gradual hearing loss. There is some controversy as to whether a minimal dysarthria is caused, but this is certainly not inevitable.

Non-verbal communication may also be affected by attempts to compensate for a hearing loss; for example, eye contact is reduced as individuals concentrate on the speaker's mouth, or proximity mores may be broken. Brinson (1983) points out that the extra demands caused by the deafness also tend to cause an inability to think beyond the immediate communication. This can lead to frustratingly slow and laboured attempts to respond in conversation.

Bernadini (1985) suggests that the teaching of communication strategies, including non-verbal skills, is an important part of the management programme for hearing-impaired individuals. This, and other aspects of aural rehabilitation, will be considered in greater depth. The role of the speech therapist in aural rehabilitation will vary enormously depending in part on situational factors (such as which other disciplines are available to the patient) and in part on personal factors (such as the therapist's level of interest, and working priorities).

Aural rehabilitation

Once a hearing loss is diagnosed, a programme must be organised which will maximise the patient's potential, within the constraints imposed by situation, service availability and personal abilities. The latter will include health, mobility and motivation, for example. Rehabilitation cannot be viewed as procedures that can be specified and generally applied, as there will be great differences between patients. However, certain principles can be stated, and it is appropriate to consider these in terms of amplification (management via the provision of aids and instruction on aid use) and of maximising communication skills. Counselling may be necessary to help an individual accept his hearing loss, and take on responsibility for his own rehabilitation. Until the loss is realistically viewed and accepted the patient will not be able to achieve the maximum benefits either from amplification or communication therapy. Chermak and Jinks (1981) point out the importance of the counsellor's own attitude towards the hearing-impaired person, which they feel is more crucial than the specific techniques or skills employed.

Amplification — provision and orientation

Once the audiometric assessment is completed, the question of aid provision must be raised. If it is decided to prescribe an aid, then the type of aid will be important. The speech therapist will not be involved directly in the choice of aid, but a knowledge of the differences between aids may be useful.

No aid has been specifically designed for elderly people, but some audiology departments have created their own adaptations to overcome some of the problems that the older person might have in using an aid. Decreased manual dexterity might mean that a small post-aural aid cannot be maintained, so a bodyworn aid is suggested, or adaptations such as fitting small handles to facilitate insertion. Body worn aids may also be suggested if more powerful amplification is needed. However, they may be cosmetically unacceptable to the patient, and if they are viewed in this way it is unlikely that the individual will persist with an orientation programme.

If the audiologist and patient can agree on the provision of a particular aid, it is essential to offer adequate counselling and follow up. Lack of this service is a false economy, as the aids provided will be less likely to be used. Sadly, few hospitals in the US or Great Britain, for example, offer this orientation programme. Blood and Danhauer (1976) in a survey in the United States, found that of 48 per cent of patients who responded eleven per cent were not using the aid provided. (It is likely that this was even higher among the 52 per cent who did not respond.) Meanwhile, Ewartson (1974) in Denmark, found a system by which all new users are trained produced only six per cent who did not wear their aids.

Orientation to the hearing aid takes time, and a programme should include explanations as to how the hearing process works, how breakdown can occur, and the effect of hearing loss. The hearing-impaired person's expectations — both of himself and of the aid — must be realistic. It must be made clear that aids have limitations, and do distort signals and amplify unwanted background noise. They are not a replacement for lost hearing.

The rehabilitation programme should involve clear explanations of how the aid works, its control and maintenance. Supervised 'trying out' of the aid is often extremely useful. There may be a few cases where a carer can be instructed to carry out aid insertion and control, on behalf of his disabled dependent, but this is not ideal.

Working through a hierarchy of listening situations can help the adjustment process, and prevents the initial shock of an aid being first worn in very noisy situations. However, it is difficult to predict who will cope with aid use, who will need extensive orientation work, and who will not cope. Schow *et al.* (1978) stated that elderly people are less likely to make a quick adjustment to wearing an aid. However, Smith and Fay (1977) found the most relevant factors (in an institutionalised population) were health, mental status and language function. Age *per se,* vision, mobility and personality were less important. Rupp, Higgins and Maurer (1977) devised a 'Feasibility scale for predicting hearing aid use with old individuals', which looks at objective information alongside the patient's own perceptions of his hearing loss.

Rehabilitation of communication skills

Hearing aid provision and orientation work will not alone be enough to achieve a hearing-impaired person's maximum potential. All possible sensory channels need to be used to reduce confusions, and thus allow the individual to function effectively both as a receiver and sender of messages.

Speech (or lip) reading, auditory training, speech conservation and non-verbal expressive skills will be important in considering communication. In addition provision of environmental aids may be useful, such as telephone attachments, television adaptors, loop systems, and advice on how to modify one's environment by, for example, using non-reverberative surrounds (carpets, absorbent tiles etc. rather than glass or metal) and reducing background noise.

Speech reading

Speech reading is a skill which has to be learnt and practised, both in optimum situations (good lighting and an unobstructed full-face view of a person speaking clearly at a reasonable rate) and in difficult situations, which are more likely to occur in the 'real world'. It will involve both drills and discussion of how to use existing knowledge of language, as a considerable amount of 'educated guesswork' is necessary in all but the most ideal situations.

Auditory training

'Learning to listen' is an important part of rehabilitation. The hearing-impaired person, of any age, will need to learn how 'to take advantage of all the acoustic clues that are still available to him' (Freestone, 1983) with amplification if it is appropriate, or without. Listening is an active process (unlike hearing) and can be practised by drillsand other methods, in different situations.

Speech conservation

The speech therapist is the most appropriate person to undertake speech conservation work, as a specialised knowledge of normal speech and voice is necessary. Rehabilitation may work on any of the segmental and suprasegmental aspects of the speech of hearing-impaired people which were mentioned earlier — voice, intonation, and so on. Parker (1983) comments on the lack of adequate research into the prevalence of speech deterioration in deafened adults, and suggests that this means that therapists should assume that all are at risk, and therefore routine speech evaluation should be carried out. At present, however, it tends to be at crisis intervention level, after intelligibility has been affected. Visual feedback techniques can be particularly helpful in teaching hearing-impaired adults (or indeed children) to maintain a good level of speech.

Non-verbal expression

The client will usually need to be taught to appreciate the value of visual clues, facial and body postures, proximity and environmental factors. These will be important both when listening and when speaking, and some may benefit from formal social skills training. Different variables are involved in different communicative situations, and these will need to be discussed — for example, use of the telephone when visual clues are not available.

Family involvement

If at all possible, family and friends should also be advised on how they can adapt to maximise the effectiveness of communication, by speaking slowly, facing the person, and so on. An advice sheet covering these suggestions is included in the appendix to Chapter 8 (p. 140). The family can play a crucial part in the rehabilitation of the hearing-impaired older person, and indeed in the pre-diagnosis period when social adjustment difficulties can arise. In institutions the staff assume the family role, and will need instructions on how to look after aids, to encourage their use, and to improve communication generally.

Organisation of rehabilitation programmes

A variety of medical and social services may be involved in the rehabilitation of older hearing-impaired people. The speech therapist will have a central role in speech conservation work, and often be part of the speech reading and auditory training programme, and in counselling.

Planning orientation programmes (even if services and equipment were available which is sadly often not the case) for older people presents various problems. Often those who may benefit have mobility problems or ill health which would prevent regular attendance at rehabilitation sessions. They may be less motivated, accepting their difficulties as part of growing old. A proportion will suffer from confusion and be unable to learn how to adjust to new aids or approaches. Such difficulties have been rather overlooked, and future planning needs not only a greater recognition of the need for aural rehabilitation programmes for all hearing impaired adults, but an awareness of the special needs of the older population.

If it is possible to work through a group sessional approach, Garstecki (1981) suggests 10–20 weekly two hour sessions, which would include a socialising time. Goals should be realistic and practical, aiming to allow the client to 'self manage problems relating to the hearing loss'. If clients cannot attend such meetings it may be possible to have a peripatetic service, working with individuals in their own homes, or to educate existing community services to explain basic information to hearing-impaired clients. If there is an involved carer then it may be best to involve them in rehabilitation work, or to advise them how to adapt their behaviours to compensate.

It is important that aural rehabilitation focuses on the overall needs of the hearing-impaired person, rather than — as has tended to happen — on one aspect such as aid provision or speech reading. This will involve a team approach, and the speech therapist will be an important member of that team.

VISION

Williamson and Caird (1986) state that 'ocular disease increases more or less exponentially with age, and thus that the very old are at a very considerable risk of one or more'. Quite apart from pathological conditions there are changes due to the aging process which may well have clinical significance in relation to the materials and approach used by speech therapists, or other clinicians working with an older population group.

Aging and vision

The structure of the human eye is shown in Figure 5.4. Good vision is the result of a focused image being produced on the retina. In older people there are structural and physiological changes that may influence vision.

Externally the eyelid tends to lose tone and elasticity, and upward (but not lowered) gaze becomes limited by atrophic changes in the elevator muscles of the eyeball. The cornea, which is the main refracting surface, may lose lustre and become more irregular. A grey ring (the arcus senilis) caused by an accumulation of lipids may be evident. Pupil size is decreased.

The anterior chamber is reduced in depth — a process that begins from the age of 25 — and the iris, in old age, becomes less permeable and depigmentation occurs. The lens grows in size and yellowing occurs, and becomes less mobile as a result of atrophy of ciliary muscles. Various opacities may form in the

Figure 5.4: Structure of the human eye

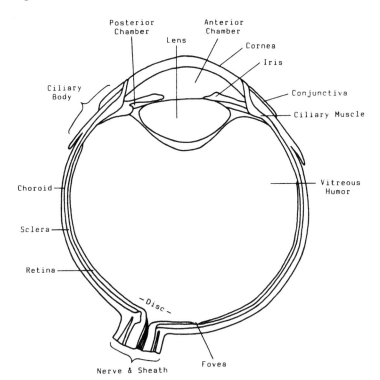

vitreous humor, which may contract away from the retina. The retina itself shows a gradual loss of neurones.

The significance of such changes are apparent in various ways. Presbyopia is common, that is, a loss of focusing power ('accommodation') which occurs up to the age of 55–60 years and then stabilises. Visual acuity, according to Marmor, Crombie and Wilson (1986) is not necessarily reduced in old age, and is, in any case, easily corrected by glasses. However more subtle visual functions do appear to weaken, and may 'alter the subjective quality of vision, even while acuity remains normal'. This is very important as there may be real visual disability despite apparently normal visual acuity.

Contrast sensitivity, which depends on the spatial presentation as well as differential brightness of stimuli, is reduced in high and middle frequencies. It may be explained by less light entering the eye and light scattering in the lens. Pattern and form perception will be affected. Adaptation is the ability to recover from changes in illumination, and may be diminished in older people, as may sensitivity to light. Older individuals are thus more susceptible to the effects of glare. Furthermore temporal factors show a degree of failure with age, and moving or sequential targets become harder to follow, and the critical flicker frequency threshold is raised.

Colour vision is affected by the gradual yellowing of the lens, which selectively absorbs and scatters blue light, while the yellow and red end of the spectrum pass unimpeded. This results in a 'perceptual increase in warm tones' and less vivid perception of blues (Marmor, 1986). Fozard *et al.* (1977) refer to loss of discrimination across the spectrum. Individual differences vary greatly however and some will have minimal colour bias as a result of aging.

A further factor to consider in discussing the effect of age on any of the senses, is the interaction between the early perceptual process and subsequent cortical functions such as decision making, memory and response processes. Perceptual judgements may be made on the basis of incomplete information, or when the incoming information is incompatible with knowledge or expectations. Older people may, as Fozard and his colleagues suggest, require more information in order to make perceptual judgements.

Visual assessment

Rennie and Davidson (1986) point out the importance of, but difficulty obtaining, a clear history from older patients. The nature of, duration and mode of onset of any visual symptoms must be established; and enquiries made as to general health, particularly considering diabetes, hypertension and other diseases known to affect vision. Drugs, and their possible ocular side effects, should be investigated.

The examination will cover visual acuity in both eyes (preferably of both distance and near vision) by using charts (such as the Snellen chart); and if necessary the pin-hole test where the patient attempts to read the chart through a pinhole to determine if there is a refractive rather than organic problem.

Pupillary reactions to light should be tested; and if there are suggestive symptoms (such as diplopia), ocular movements assessed.

External examination of the periocular tissues, eyelids, cornea and conjuctiva may reveal problems particularly in older patients, and intra-ocular pressure should always be measured. Ophthalmoscopy allows the ocular media and fundi to be assessed, but elderly patients often present with dense lens opacities which make examination of the fundus impossible. In this case retinal and macular function will be evaluated.

Visual fields may be tested by the confrontation method, but this tends only to disclose gross defects (usually those of neurological origin), as Rennie and Davidson point out. If a defect is suspected perimetry may be used to confirm it. There may be a specific distortion of the central field of vision affecting shape or size of the image, and this may be tested by using the Amsler Grid. There are various texts which will more fully explain the methods and materials used to assess vision, but in general the speech therapist will not need a detailed knowledge of these.

Problems assessing the older person's vision

As with auditory assessment there are difficulties in completing a comprehensive assessment of vision. Memory loss may, for example, make it difficult to obtain a full history of the visual symptoms. Mental or physical disorder may mean a person is incapable of tests that involve more complex instructions or fine motor control.

Difficulty attending clinic may be an obstacle, as in hearing testing, and similarly the tendency of older people to respond overcautiously.

Visual problems common in an elderly population

There are various conditions that affect the eye and/or vision, and which are more prevalent in older age groups. Glaucoma, for example, while not intrinsically related to aging has a higher incidence in the older population. The glaucomas are a group of diseases characterised by raised intra-ocular pressure, and due to impaired drainage of aqueous humour. Visual acuity often remains good until late in the course of the disease, but there are visual field losses. Despite medical and surgical treatments glaucoma remains a common cause of blindness.

Cataracts result in a loss of lens transparency, and the most common symptom is failing vision. The specific consequences depend on the anatomical sites involved — they may be cortical, nuclear, capsular or subcapsular (Crombie, 1986). They affect about 18 per cent of people in their 70s and 36 per cent of those over 80 years old (Fozard *et al.*, 1977). Treatment is by surgical removal of the cataract, and general ill health may contraindicate such an operation. The majority of cataract extractions are successful but there are not uncommonly complications either during or after the operation itself. Crombie points out that older patients will often take longer to return to normal, and need extra support.

Macular disease affects detail vision, and accounts for 45 per cent of visual problems in older people (Gordon, 1965). Diabetic retinopathy is more likely in early onset diabetes but can occur in older individuals. The retina may become detached, as a result of diabetes or of fluid collection or any space occupying lesion. There are obviously numerous other conditions affecting the eye and vision in older people, and a good summary is provided by Caird and Williamson (1986).

Psychosocial effects of visual impairment

'In the elderly vision is principally needed to maintain a home and, so far as other disabilities permit, to preserve independence and to attend to one's personal needs' (Wilson, 1986). Visual impairment in older people is usually of gradual onset, and help is often not sought as it is accepted as part of growing old. The psychological impact of a loss of vision can be enormous, however, having far-reaching effects in most facets of life. Shopping, reading, writing and driving, for example, will obviously be affected. The visually impaired will be less mobile, and a vicious cycle may be set up as confidence is lost.

Blindness will often be a terrifying experience, isolating individuals and imprisoning them in their homes. Older people, with fewer reasons perhaps to make an effort to go out, and who may for mental or physical reasons be less able to adjust, will suffer as much as younger blind people but often with fewer resources available to them, or of which they can make use.

Vision and communication

The obvious way in which visual impairment may affect communication is in relation to the written word, that is, reading and writing become difficult or impossible. However, the impact of a lessened ability to see and make use of non-verbal cues is grossly underrated. It may lead to misunderstandings at times, or effectively block the reception of a message. Nuances of meaning will be lost, for example when a facial expression is used to convey a meaning which is incongruent with the simultaneous verbal message. It will, at times, cause an older person to be put at risk — if they are unable to read instructions or warnings on medicines, for instance.

The fact that the sense of touch and hearing are also more likely to be impaired as people grow older also means that a visual impairment may close doors in terms of rehabilitation and adjustment. No longer could visual channels be used to compensate for impaired hearing, for instance.

Rehabilitation

The first stage in rehabilitation is to determine whether glasses will be useful, and if so provide them. Instead of, or in addition to, glasses other low vision aids (such as magnifying glasses) may be suggested.

Adapted reading material (bearing in mind that good contrast is more important than high magnification) is available — large print books are in most libraries, and often organisations for the blind produce news and magazine programmes on tape. Lighting must be good, and free from glare — Wilson suggests that a multiposition lamp with an opaque shade is the best option.

The speech therapist will not normally be involved in the primary management of a visual impairment. However, she will frequently find older patients referred who have visual difficulties in addition to a specific speech or language impairment. On an even more basic level changes in vision that are part of the aging process may well affect a person's ability to respond to and make use of traditional assessment and therapy material — colour vision, for example.

If there is an impairment of vision that channel will not be possible for the therapist to suggest to compensate for a language or speech disorder, and it can be extremely difficult to prepare a management programme which is both positive and realistic for such patients.

In a more general, indirect way the speech therapist may be the most able person to teach other professionals how vision is important to communication, and how to compensate for any visual handicap. There is no doubt that much more work needs to be done in this field, and that speech therapists — particularly those working with an older population — should be more concerned with the effects of visual impairment.

AGING AND SOMAESTHESIS/TASTE/SMELL

Although little work has been done on how the other senses are affected by the aging process, it is worth noting that there does seem to be a decrease in touch, vibration, temperature, kinaesthesis and pain sensitivity (Kenshalo, 1977). Such changes are not, however, inevitable and may be explained by neuropathies rather than age *per se*. Central neurological processes may explain difficulties in administering and interpreting complex tests of sensory function. Engen (1977), in his review of research into taste and smell found little available information, but a suggestion that taste sensitivity may decline, but smell seems stable. Individual preferences may be more significant than has been hitherto accepted.

Communication may be affected by decreased sensitivity or an impairment of touch; but effects will probably only be great if other sensory avenues which more commonly serve a communicative function are also impaired. There is no evidence that if touch is the medium by which an individual communicates (for example in the case of blind and deaf people) aging will impair this sufficiently for it to create a functionally significant communication problem.

6

Hospital and Community

Earlier chapters have described some of the more common communication difficulties found in an adult, and specifically older adult, population. A major factor influencing their adjustment, and the way in which the speech therapist will plan management, is the environment within which they live. Some communication difficulties may be compounded, or indeed caused, by the individual's environment, but similarly, the setting can encourage rehabilitation attempts. This chapter will attempt to describe the different environments in which elderly people are found, and specifically to discuss the role of the speech therapist in hospital and in the community. Institutional life, whether in long-stay hospitals or in old people's homes, creates a very particular environment, and the inherent problems of such settings will be covered in Chapter 7.

Figure 6.1 lists the different living environments of elderly people, along a spectrum or continuum of dependency. The more independent will live at home, perhaps with the support of domiciliary services or day care; the more dependent and therefore less able will often be placed in residential or hospital care. Often different terminology is employed (for example, in the United States and in Great Britain), but different labels mask similar facilities. There is, however, between hospitalisation and independent life, a separation which has created a 'no-mans land' in care provision, with many elderly falling into the 'too fit but too frail' category. That is, they are too fit for hospitalisation to be necessary, but too frail to cope independently. This gap is filled to some extent by privately run or state-funded nursing homes. Sadly, however, it remains true that many elderly people, who need some degree of nursing

95

Figure 6.1: The continuum of care/services for elderly people

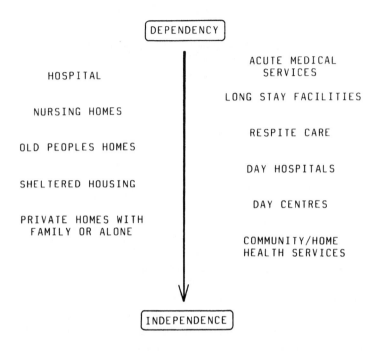

care, end up in long-stay hospital wards quite inappropriately, because the appropriate alternative does not exist.

The current trend is towards returning individuals to the community, or maintaining people at home in order to prevent the need for admission to hospital. Preventive care, based on early education, may in future years mitigate or delay some of the functional difficulties of old age. The efficacy of applying preventive medical care to the already aged is dubious, being influenced, as Kane, Kane and Arnold (1985) suggest, by the 'narrow therapeutic window that characterises the elderly person'.

CARE/SERVICES FOR ELDERLY PEOPLE

Hospital facilities and other residential care

The 'fit elderly' will often receive acute medical care on general hospital wards. Those who are often described as 'geriatric', being physiologically aged and frequently suffering from multiple pathologies, will often be admitted to geriatric wards or units for rehabilitation or maintenance. There are signs that such segregated units may decline, with an increasing number of voices supporting the need to integrate elderly people into general wards. The trend to community care has resulted in a less-able population of older people in hospitals and residential homes; and the mix of frail and confused often presents a depressing picture to outsiders, and indeed to the staff and patients themselves. Integration may go some way towards improving the image of the dependent elderly person.

The role of the chronic long-stay hospital may also be taken by nursing home facilities which are able to provide skilled nursing care. These nursing homes vary enormously in standards and in size, and face similar problems to the hospitals, including the risk of institutionalising residents. Old people's homes may be run privately, by voluntary bodies, or by the state. They do not provide nursing care, and are therefore intended for a more independent population, although the borderline has become increasingly blurred. Admission criteria differ greatly between countries, and even between individual facilities, but increasing numbers of hospitals, nursing homes and old people's homes also now provide respite care, offering short admissions to enable the carer to have a break from the day to day burdens and responsibilities of his or her role.

Day care provision

Hospital day care services for the elderly population were first established in Oxford, UK in 1958, and have proved a useful adjunct to more traditional hospital treatment. Brocklehurst and Tucker (1980) describe the functions of a geriatric day hospital as 'rehabilitation, maintenance assessment, medical, nursing and social care'. Such a facility must operate within a comprehensive geriatric service. They found, contrary to expectations, that relatively few became chronic attenders, and thus the balance of places was not disrupted. However, it may be that some attenders gain no benefit from a geriatric day hospital, that would not be gained from more traditional outpatient work, so it is important that the criteria for admission are specified.

There may also be, in addition to hospital-based day care facilities, social service and voluntary day centres. These usually provide no trained medical or nursing care, but operate as a social/rehabilitative outlet. Such facilities are not always available; for example the United States did not follow Britain in making day care provision until very much later, and there are still states who have not legislated on day care. However, this service is becoming more and more important, and the demands placed upon it must eventually result in increased provision. As more people are maintained in the community, day care will often be the vital ingredient preventing hospital admission.

Sheltered housing

Sheltered housing describes schemes where individuals or couples are able to live independently in their own flats, but have the added security of a resident warden on call. Each flat is provided with emergency call buttons which can be operated if help is needed. Such developments are becoming increasingly popular, and may be run by social services or private schemes. Often flats are in purpose-built buildings or developmental areas, but there is also a limited number of peripatetic wardens, who cover those people at risk who live within a specified catchment zone.

Community or home health services

Community services aim to provide health and supportive care to sick or disabled people in their own homes. The level of care necessary will vary greatly, and in each case certain disciplines will or will not be needed.

It should be stressed that an overwhelming majority of elderly people live in private housing, either alone or with relatives. Community services can enable many to remain at home, both by directly supporting the patient, and also by offering a degree of physical and psychological support to the carer. It is very often the case that the financial and other burdens of caring fall upon the family, and it is certain that the social and health services could not cope with care of the older population were family support withdrawn. It makes both economic and human sense; therefore, to offer as much support as possible to these carers, domiciliary services are now a priority, and may be able to maintain people at home despite extreme levels of physical disability.

The services that may be wheeled into action on a domiciliary basis are numerous. They include the general practitioner or family doctor; district nurse, health visitor, geriatric nurse visitor, social worker, home help, occupational therapist, physiotherapist, speech therapist, chiropodist and various voluntary agencies. One problem in the community is that there seems to be an ever-growing number of disciplines and individuals involved, and often their role is not clearly defined. In addition, elderly clients change in terms of functional ability and needs relatively quickly, and therefore constant review is essential. Community rehabilitation does, as Webster and Webster (1977) point out, provide 'a challenge to rethink accepted roles'. A later chapter will concentrate on the role of the multidisciplinary team.

Community services are stretched, and it is important therefore that this limited facility reaches those who are most in need. Morris, Sherwood and Mor (1984) describe an assessment tool (The Hebrew Rehabilitation Center for The Aged Vulnerability Index) which attempts to identify functionally at risk persons in the community, while avoiding long and expensive multidisciplinary assessments, by asking ten questions relating to household chores and needs, mobility and activity level.

A continuing problem in working with older people in any setting is that few disciplines include comprehensive education about the aging client within their recognised training courses. Individuals are expected to pick up the relevant knowledge and skills 'as they go', and speech therapy is no exception.

THE ROLE OF THE SPEECH THERAPIST

Elderly people in hospital

A questionnaire distributed in Great Britain, in 1977, found that geriatric patients were seen by speech therapists in three different work places — geriatric hospitals or day centres (17 per cent), geriatric units within general hospitals (73 per cent) or speech therapy departments, having been placed on acute hospital wards (10 per cent) (Cox and Swan, 1978). The same study found that the speech therapist involved herself in the broad field of communication problems of the elderly population (including the effects of institutionalisation) only when appointed to a unit independent of general hospital work. In the latter, therapists tend to respond only to specific referrals, probably as a result of workload and case priorities.

The aims of, and therefore the method of, treatment will differ depending on the overall management goals for each patient. If the person is being prepared for discharge, the speech therapy programme must take into account the person's needs once he has been returned to the community. It is rare for a speech therapist to accompany older patients on trial home visits — as the occupational therapist may — but this could be a valuable assessment procedure. Indeed it may markedly alter the direction of therapy.

Conversely if the individual is likely to remain in long-term institutional care, he will have different needs, not least of which is the provision of an environment that encourages rehabilitation and communication. There is increasing awareness among speech therapists of the need to be more pragmatic in planning and carrying out management programmes.

One difficulty in hospital work is finding the best location in which to see older patients. Properly to assess and treat will necessitate observation on the ward, rather than automatic transfer to the speech therapy department. Once the needs of the individual in the ward setting have been assessed, ideally a treatment room on or near the ward may be used, as treatment is difficult actually on the ward with the surroundings bustle of the nursing routines. If treatment can be based within the ward, however, it may be possible to involve staff, who are in the role of carers and often of 'primary communication partner' — that is, the people with whom the older person is most likely to attempt to communicate. However, staff are notoriously hard to recruit for geriatric units, and low staff–patient ratios mean there is frequently no-one available to become involved in treatment programmes outside specific nursing duties. It is important that speech therapists are realistic in approaching other staff, and in their expectations of them. Too often, therapists act as if other staff should immediately respond, and be prepared to undertake work on their behalf.

It is true that staff on geriatric units often hold somewhat negative attitudes towards rehabilitation. One reason for this is a deeply ingrained belief in the medical model, which aims to cure. Such an aim is unrealistic with many so-called geriatric patients, and therefore medical staff veto referrals to speech therapy, feeling that the patient cannot be 'improved'. The role of the speech therapist in maintaining communication skills, and in maximising residual potential is much more relevant on a typical geriatric unit, than is the 'curative' or 'improving' role when specific advances in speech or language skills are the goal.

Most speech therapists who have elderly clients who are not hospitalised are still seeing them within a hospital setting. However, as general medical care drifts away from the hospital to the community, so there are more opportunities for speech and language clinicians to become involved with this population in their own homes, rather than bringing them in to the hospital for out-patient appointments. As some communication difficulties, or elements of such conditions, can be a function of the individual's environment, attempting to evaluate outside that environment can be, at the least, misleading, and can lead to wrong clinical decisions.

Elderly people at home

More than 80 per cent of the over 65-year-old population live in their own or family homes in the community. They tend to have poorer housing, often in bad repair, and often under-occupied (Kellaher, Peace and Willcocks, 1985). Many endure enforced isolation as a result of poor mobility, loss of family and friends, poor health and sensory losses. Those who live with others find that, as they age and their role within the household changes, so the communication patterns within the family alter. If the older person is physically or mentally unwell, he and the carers face additional difficulties. Communication may suffer in quantity and quality, and there will also be a change in relationships. The mother, for example, is no longer viewed as the nurturer and 'giver', but becomes a dependent, a 'taker'. The father loses his position as head of household, and breadwinner. All the members of the family must rethink their position within that unit.

Communication impairment in a dependent older relation is

more likely to lead a family to consider residential care for that person, than is a physical illness, even if it necessitates quite substantial nursing care.

In summary, therefore, the older person at home may face communication difficulties as a result of isolation, or of family adjustment problems, whether or not there is also a specific communication disorder. If there is, for example, an aphasia or dysarthria the former factors may well compound the degree of handicap due to the specific problem.

Cox and Swan (1978) found that although 62 per cent of their small sample of therapists working in geriatric units did make home visits, most did so because of transport difficulties rather than as a chosen method of working. Of the 31 therapists making domiciliary visits, 86 per cent visited to carry out assessment, 58 per cent to offer some therapy, and 70 per cent as follow-up visits. It is to be hoped that the trend towards a more functional approach to the rehabilitation of communication disorders is reflected in an increase in those therapists who would see domiciliary work as a treatment of choice.

The advantages of home-based therapy

Assessment and needs

The patient with a speech or language disorder will usually benefit if assessment and treatment can take place within the environment in which they must function on a daily basis. Therapy can then base on his or her needs, rather than on artificial clinical measures. People behave very differently when they attend a hospital clinic, and they also relate differently to relatives. Thus even if relatives attend a clinic with the patient, the therapist will not gain a true picture of the family's communication patterns. The perceptions held by patient and family of the communication disorder, and its effects on their lifestyle are important, but may not appear to relate to the objective situation. Observation in the home may help the therapist to counsel the family in order to achieve this balance, and regain some of the stability lost with the original crisis situation. Thus, home visiting can facilitate identification of environmental factors affecting communication (Lubinski, 1984).

Materials

Home-based therapy (which would include seeing residents of old people's homes in those homes) also allows materials and props to be used, which have meaning for the patient. Mementoes and photographs, for example, can be potent conversation pieces. Wallace and Canter (1985) addressed this question, feeling that there was a need for empirical rather than anecdotal evidence that using personally relevant language materials leads to better communication. Their work bore out the hypothesis, bearing in mind that their group was small and only looked at certain tasks. It is not, as they point out, possible to say whether it is the personal nature of the items, or the frequency with which they 'occur', or the effect of greater motivation that leads to the end result. Clinically, the cause is less important than the effect.

The family

The therapist can involve the family in the process of rehabilitation more easily at home, and can act as model and as counsellor to improve the communicative relationships within the family. The family also are allowed to act as host, rather than being limited to the 'taker's' role. Many will be more relaxed, and more confident about asking questions or giving an opinion. Others who visit the home (lay or professional callers) regularly can also be involved via explanations and advice. All too often, techniques that work in the clinic are not effectively communicated to others with whom the patient has contact outside that setting.

Transport

Transport is a perennial problem for all out-patient services, but especially for those, like speech therapy, which are considered non-priority. Even when ambulance services are booked they tend to involve long waits, and disrupted therapy time. Elderly patients may be frail, and are often too exhausted, anxious or disoriented when they arrive at the clinic to be able to benefit from treatment. There are also those who are unable to travel to hospital, and who have often 'slipped the net' in terms of speech therapy provision. Finally, there are those who refuse to travel to the hospital, but are willing to co-operate in home-based therapy programmes. However, Stevens (1985b), in discussing the question of transport, points out that there are those who can travel and might in fact benefit from a change in environment. Such people would be encouraged to attend as out-patients.

The 'sick role'

Continual hospital appointments can tend to promote and prolong the idea of illness, thus impeding progress and adjustment. In these cases, a domiciliary service can lessen the individual's dependency on the sick role, a point Stevens (1985b) also makes.

Economics

In small geographical areas, the provision of a community speech therapy service to adults can be cost effective. Ambulance transport costs are high, and mileage expenses for the short distances involved for the speech therapist will be considerably lower.

The disadvantages of home-based therapy

Many of the advantages have the potential of becoming disadvantages.

Assessment needs

While the strongest argument for domiciliary work is the fact that it is more functionally based and patient-centred, there are households where distractions are rife, and the necessary degree of organisation cannot be established. Usually a suitable environment can be created, but it may occasionally take some time.

Materials

The therapist must plan materials carefully, and 'work in' to the plan for each session a degree of flexibility, to ensure the necessary materials are taken to or available in the patient's home. Certain materials and assessment instruments will be difficult or impossible to transport from the clinic, and in such cases the therapist must weigh the benefits of being able to use that equipment against those incurred as a result of seeing the patient at home.

The family

While some families help, others can hinder progress, and be 'disruptive and defensive' (Lubinski, 1981a). This may not be a deliberate policy of non-cooperation, but many close relationships will not support an alteration in roles which involves one becoming the 'teacher' and one the 'pupil'. The therapist will need sensitively to assess the individual situation, and remember that criticism is often hardest to take from those closest to the person.

Transport/economics

While ambulance costs may be cut, the therapist may have to travel long distances, particularly in large rural areas and will be forced to spend a considerable proportion of time travelling. The size of the therapist's catchment area may well be a relevant factor in whether a domiciliary service is economically viable. Time spent travelling also means fewer patients can be seen, and in the event of a patient being unable to participate in therapy and failing to cancel an appointment there is little to fill the time wasted. In the clinic, most therapists have pressing administration or planning work to cover failed appointments. It can also be difficult to contact patients if the therapist is unable to visit, or is forced to change appointment times.

Public relations

A great barrier to developing a comprehensive community service for the speech and language disordered is the way in which the speech therapist's role is perceived by the general public. Of all the remedial professions, it seems that the least is known about speech therapy.

The basic aims for the patient in hospital or community are to enable him or her to communicate needs, and beyond that, to achieve a level of communication that maximises his potential and/or is acceptable to him. Different physical and social environments will lead to different goals and motivations. The need to restore a desire, and the opportunity, to communicate may need to be an initial focus in working with the elderly in hospital, residential care or at home.

THE HOSPITAL–COMMUNITY BARRIER

The gap in care between hospital medical and nursing care, and the community provision has already been remarked upon. This gap has frequently been a barrier to the development of effective and comprehensive care of older people. Many are discharged from hospital without adequate follow-up in the community which often leads to rapid readmission. Communicatively impaired people may similarly fail to receive adequate follow-up care on discharge, and at this point in treatment may 'slip through the net' and are left to cope alone. Those who did not require hospital care may also fail to be seen by speech therapists, as a result of poor liaison with family doctors and other community services, and their failure to refer if they feel there is likely to be little specific improvement in speech or language.

A hospital-based community speech therapist can be a useful bridge, enabling patients to be seen after discharge if unable to attend out-patient clinics. Such a post also forges yet another link between health and social services, and places the therapist in a position from which he or she can be involved in educating the public about the role of speech therapy.

7

The Institutional Environment

The interdependence of communication and the environment was briefly touched upon in Chapter 6, in stressing the need to assess and treat communicatively impaired individuals within their normal environment. Environmental factors will influence with whom, when and how people communicate, as well as affecting other behaviours. Powell-Lawton (1977) describes an 'optimal environment' as one in which the person's needs are met by their physical and social environment. Attempts to maximise the level of congruence between needs and environment will affect the individual's behaviours. This can be specifically applied to communication needs, and how the physical and social environment helps or hinders the communicative process.

The physical environment is the sum of those potentially changeable physical factors in any situation (such as the layout of furniture) and of the unchangeable (such as shape and size of rooms, and the external climate). The social environment refers to the existence of potential communication partners. It is the individual's perception of this potential, not the mere existence of other people, that is important.

It will be immediately obvious that the institutional environment is a very particular one, both in physical and social terms. Those elderly people living in institutions will also face a social environment which has altered as a function of aging — in the loss of close friends and relations, for example. It also seems likely that the older person's perceptions of his environment will be affected not just by personality, but also by the sensoriperceptual changes brought about by the aging process.

INSTITUTIONAL LIFE

In the United States approximately five per cent of over 65-year-olds live in residential settings, for a variety of physical, mental and social reasons. Thus the majority still live in the community, but for those others institutional life necessitates an enormous change in their situation. Although the trend, commented on by Bennett (1963), towards institutionalisation seems to have been reversed, those who do still make this move ('relocation') rarely meet the sensitive handling that the situation warrants.

Relocation

When a person leaves his own home to live in an institution, however well run, he faces a very real adjustment problem. This is evidenced by the increase in the mortality and morbidity rates among relocated elderly people. Ainsworth (1977) for example, reported a mortality rate of 32 per cent, compared with 19 per cent of a matched control group. It may be that the newness of the environment is perceived as a threat, or that each must process more information in order to function safely in a strange setting.

Relocation effects of separation, rejection, loss and despair are common, and can compound other adjustment problems that an individual faces in accepting aging, or in accepting bereavement, illness or handicap. Both the older person and his family will need sensitive counselling to enable them to face the decision to go into residential care, and to carry out that decision once made.

Kellaher, Pearce and Wilcocks (1985) attempted to summarise the pros and cons of moving into an old people's home (Table 7.1). They discuss the difficulties inherent in the situation in which there is enforced contact with 'complete strangers in unfamiliar public settings', often made worse by institutional decor and furnishings. If there is a feeling of having been manipulated into the move, either by family or by official agencies, the settling-in period will be even more difficult.

Most of the reasons for moving into a home can be looked at from two angles. For example, there is the advantage of the removal of much of the burden of coping, but nothing is

Table 7.1: Coping with institutional life

Pros	Cons
Burden of coping removed	Removal of structure and resulting apathy
Opportunity for social contact	Loss of privacy (and expectation one should 'join in')
Removal of anxiety and risks	Loss of independence
Finances sorted out	Loss of control
Regular health attention	Depressing picture of ability levels
Relationship with family may ease	Less contact with family and little opportunity for privacy on visits
Improved physical care — warmth, repair of buildings etc.	Sense of loss on giving up home and personal possessions

Source: Based on Kellaher *et al.* (1985)

provided to take the place of coping activities. There are fewer risks to face, and there is opportunity for more social contact. However, the loss of privacy, independence and control weigh heavily against these advantages.

Characteristics of institutional life

Institutions develop their own 'specific way of life to which inmates are socialised and expected to adjust' (Bennett, 1963). Thus, individuals find themselves expected to learn to adapt to new roles and rules. Kleemeier (1959) identified three dominant characteristics of institutions: (1) the extent to which they are integrated within the larger society (segregate dimension); (2) the extent to which residents are involved in the same routines (congregate dimension); and (3) the extent to which behaviour is standardised by the attitudes and approach of staff (control dimension). These three dimensions often produce an 'encompassing, restrictive and artificial life style, in which people who are not related, nor have first established a close relationship, are required to live together in close proximity' (Nuru, 1985).

THE INSTITUTIONAL ENVIRONMENT

The unwritten rules of institutional life, and the expectation that people will conform, are strong enough to ensure that few attempt to break the mould, and assume their own routine out of line with that of the institution. Goffman (1960) talked of two mutually exclusive systems — the staff and the residents. The expectations of the higher ranking staff group are rationalised by the residents. Newcomers then use the older residents as role models, and thus expectations are transmitted.

While these unfavourable features of institutional life are true, there is also the fact that there are enormous difficulties in running homes. Not least of these is the role of old people's homes in dealing with a heterogeneous population, many of whom have special needs. Other limiting factors include financial considerations, and staff recruitment and turnover.

The communicative environment

Lubinski (1984) has coined the term 'The Communicative Environment' to refer to the relationship between the elderly person in an institution and his environment. Successful communication is 'the feeling of fulfilment gained when a message is sent and received'. It allows the individual to remain an active interactor, but it is only possible when the environment encourages such interchange.

A 'communication impaired environment' is found in many institutions. While accepting that there will be differences in communication needs and behaviour because of the nature of the people and setting, there are still unnecessary hindrances and obstacles to successful communication. This 'communication impaired environment' is described by Lubinski as 'a setting in which there are few opportunities available for successful, meaningful communication'. Such a setting has rules, albeit unwritten ones, about where, when, to whom and about what residents may communicate, and give little in the way of reasons to talk, as the environment is so static. There is little opportunity for privacy, staff do not value nor reinforce communication, and residents themselves contribute to the picture — 'each feeling unique in a world of the senile, dying and ill'. The physical design and decor further add to this depressing situation. Obviously not all these obstacles exist in all homes, but they are common rather than uncommon.

110

Furthermore, the individual's experiences and needs will affect the degree to which he or she is affected by the environment.

Lubinski (1981a) writes 'The improvement of communication skills and opportunities of older individuals in all settings must be considered a right and not a privilege, a priority and not a by-product, and a reality not an ideal'. In no setting is this more true than in institutional care.

Staff views on communication

Staff tend to feel the better-adjusted residents are those who conform, and there are often approval-based sanctions. Bennett (1963) found that both staff and residents expected the latter not to complain, to keep active, to avoid arguments, and to avoid intimate contacts. There is also some evidence of racially based distinctions — Weinstock and Bennett (1968) found different patterns of communication between white and black residents and staff.

Few care staff in homes are offered explanations and information about communication, and therefore do not value its role in personal fulfilment. Many see the priority as the physical caring, and find it hard to appreciate the need to balance this with the emotional needs of their resident group. When staff have been involved in encouraging verbal inter-action, and trained accordingly, increased amounts of verbalisa-tion have been noted (Lubinski, 1978–79). One problem with care staff in institutions is that they are often perceived by outsiders as being less capable of 'better work' and this stereotype can itself lead staff to resent their work.

When staff do attempt to communicate, much has been written about the tendency to use 'baby talk' to older people, and most view this in a poor light. However, various researchers have found that such language is viewed as conveying reassur-ance and nurturance to those of lower functional ability. One problem is the danger that, by talking in this way to people of whom they expect less, they may create self-fulfilling prophesies, influencing the status of those residents (Caporael, Lukaszewski and Cuthbertson, 1983). Certainly it would be considered perjorative to talk in this manner to all residents, regardless of their ability level, and this does happen.

THE INSTITUTIONAL ENVIRONMENT

Residents' views on communication

While most of the limited research on communication in institutions has looked at it from the angle of staff viewpoints, or physical setting, Lubinski, Morrison and Rigrodsky (1981) interviewed residents to obtain their views. Their subjects were chronically ill elderly residents, who were interviewed about the quantity, content and locale of communication, and about their

Table 7.2: Attitudes of elderly institutionalised patients to communication

(i) Patient responses to questions on quantity of communication

	Number responding	
Question	Average amount or more	Very little
How much do residents talk with each other?	17	7
How much do residents talk in the hallways?	0	24
How much do you talk with other residents?	4	20
How much do you talk with your roommate?	0	20 *
How much do you talk with staff members?	10	10 **

*   Four patients had no roommate
** Four patients did not respond

(ii) Patient responses to questions regarding their communication partners

	Question		
Person	Most frequent partner	Partners to avoid	Desired partners
People off the floor	4	0	0
People on floor (not roommate)	8	0	0
Roommate	1	20	0
Those with particular characteristics	8	17	12
Speech impaired	0	8	0
Staff	0	0	2
Family	0	0	0
No one	3	5	8

112

THE INSTITUTIONAL ENVIRONMENT

(iii) Patient responses to questions regarding the content of their communication

Content	Current topics with patients	Current topics with staff	Desired topics
Trivia/social amenities	5	4	0
Health and medication	2	22	0
Home and family	5	0	0
Hospital activities	1	0	0
Personal interests	7	0	16
Food and eating	15	0	0
'Anything'	6	1	0
Nothing	0	0	3

(iv) Patient responses to questions regarding the places where communication occurs

	Question	
Places	Frequently occurs in	Places to avoid
Public	22	15
Private	2	0
No place	0	0
No responses	0	9

(v) Patient responses to questions regarding communicative desire and enjoyment

Question	Yes	No	No response
Do you like to talk?	13	9	2
Do you enjoy talking?	19	3	2

Source: Lubinski, R. Perception of spoken communication by elderly chronically ill patients in institutional setting. *Journal of Speech and Hearing Disorders, 46.* November 1981. Copyright 1981 the American Speech–Language–Hearing Association, Rockville, Maryland, USA.

communication partners. Some of their responses can be found in Table 7.2.

The admittedly small number of subjects felt that various influences were operating on their communicative behaviours, either to hinder or to encourage interaction. These influences included personal characteristics, staff characteristics, interests, health, rules within institutional life, privacy and proximity to other residents at different times of the day. The authors

113

interpreted their findings as representing two conflicts which inhibited even those residents who wanted to talk. One conflict was of approach-avoidance, characterised by the resident's limiting his or her own opportunities by being selective about partners, and by fearing gossip and disappointment within close relationships. The second conflict was of approach-inhibition, where communication is limited by the institutional characteristics of lack of privacy, adoption of the 'patient-resident' role, lack of activity, and by mores established by staff and rationalised as maintaining a serene environment.

In summary, it appears that while staff may be less positive than are the residents about the latter's abilities, both groups perceive communication as limited and of little or no value. The continuation of negative conditions is thus the result of a vicious circle of psychological, social and physical factors.

ASSESSING COMMUNICATION IN INSTITUTIONS

There are difficulties in differential diagnosis of elderly institutionalised patients' communication disorders. In addition to considering the effects of the normal aging process, the speech therapist must decide the degree of influence of physical, psychological and institutional factors. Lubinski feels that 'identifying the cause of the problem becomes less crucial than delineating the symptoms, and planning a feasible and effective therapeutic program'. Certainly, it is important to plan effective individual therapy, but if the cause or partial cause is environmental, this needs to be known in order to remove the handicapping factors; symptomatic therapy will not be sufficient to prevent the difficulties recurring if they stem from environmental causes.

One problem is that no tests have been designed to look at the communicative needs and behaviours of the institutionalised. The CADL assessment (Holland, 1980) has been administered to institutionalised elderly people, and found lower scores than for non-institutionalised controls. Similarly, Russell (1981) found lowered percentile scores using the Porch Index of Communicative Ability (PICA) for the residents of old peoples' homes, compared to independent and day centre subjects. If norms were obtained on such tests it would serve to lower expectations of residents in old peoples' homes, and in any case these assessments may not be most appropriate either in general for elderly people, or when taken out of their country of origin. It is more important that a specific method of assessing this particular population is compiled. Such an assessment should consider the patient-resident, the staff and the physical setting. Keenan (1979) did attempt to look at this problem, and included the patients' perceptions of their conversation, and assessment of physical, psychological and environmental influences. Adelson *et al.* (1982) meanwhile, looked at staff ('health professionals') interactions with aged patients, and found the best supervisors used more banter and chat, combined with information giving, use of the resident's name, and requests for feedback. Such staff may be used as role models in training other professionals interacting with elderly people, who may then be assessed on these parameters.

Some of the questions which may be useful for the speech-language therapist to ask about communication in old peoples' homes are listed in Appendix 7.1 (p. 126).

It may not be possible to eliminate possible causes of a communicative disorder until a period of diagnostic therapy has been undertaken, or until any improvement is noticed following on from environmental modification. Therapists need to identify which individuals will benefit most from direct intervention. O'Connell and O'Connell (1978) found that 70 per cent of their patients, within a skilled nursing facility, made little or no improvement. If a method can be found of determining what criteria make a person suitable for direct intervention within an institutional setting, it could prevent a considerable misuse of therapist time.

The speech therapist, however, has an important role in institutions for elderly people, not just in working with individuals who have speech or language disorders, but in attacking the features of institutional life that limit the residents' communication attempts and skills. This might include becoming involved in education programmes, altering physical surroundings, and running groups.

THE SPEECH AND LANGUAGE DISORDERED IN INSTITUTIONS

The influence of institutional life on the residents' opportunities,

THE INSTITUTIONAL ENVIRONMENT

desires and abilities to communicate will often compound the communicatively disordered individual's difficulties.

One study, backed by the US Public Health Service Office (1975), quoted figures of approximately 33 per cent of residents in long-term care who had speech and/or language problems, and another 33 per cent with hearing loss. Bloomer (1960) found that 45 per cent of residents in a county hospital facility had speech/language impairments. Others have quoted figures as high as 56 per cent (Page, 1967), 60 per cent (Mueller and Peters, 1981) and the 92.5 per cent of Chaffee's (1967) sample who required 'special staff consideration with regard to speech and hearing'. Table 7.3 shows the findings of a small pilot study in two state-run homes in London, which found 41 per cent of residents to have a communication disorder which was sufficient to impair functional ability.

Table 7.3: Incidence of speech/language disorders in two old peoples' homes

	Percentage of residents
(a) Ages	
55 to 65	1.0
65 to 75	15.0
75 to 85	53.5
85 to 95	26.5
95 +	4.0
(b) Communication disorder	
Dysphasia	4.5
Language of dementia	17.5
Dysarthria	11.0
Dysphonia	6.5
Dysfluency	1.5

It has already been mentioned that not all could benefit from direct speech therapy intervention as O'Connell and O'Connell discovered. Mueller and Peters (1981), however, felt that 48 per cent of their sample could be helped in this way. If individuals are felt to be suitable, the speech therapist's role will be as with other communicatively impaired older patients. As their home is the institution, it will be useful if they can be treated within that environment, and if staff can be involved in advice and counselling work. Aims must realistically reflect the fact that

116

institutionalisation factors will not disappear overnight, and also that there will be functional differences between communication in institutions and in the 'outside world'. It may be that unnecessary effort and time has been spent on trying to make them the same inappropriately. Any ultra supportive environment, such as an institution for elderly people, will decrease communicative needs on certain levels.

The dementing resident

There is a large proportion of residents in chronic long-stay wards of hospitals, or in old peoples' homes, who are dementing, and have resulting communication difficulties. This proportion is increasing as the level of functional ability of residents is falling as a result of general trends in health care.

There is a danger in institutions that an early label is applied, and sticks, even without medical diagnosis to support the labelling. New residents, who understandably show signs of confusion in a new and strange environment, are thus dismissed as 'dements'. The application of such a label often leads to a 'cycle of incompetence' (Lubinski, 1984). Staff respond to the label, expect less of the individual and the resident begins to fulfil their expectations, becoming less motivated and more dependent. Thus, negative functioning spirals as a result of these self-fulfilling prophesies. People talk differently to those who are labelled demented, using 'secondary baby talk', and also tend to respond to residents as if their level of communication skill inevitably reflects their mental capabilities.

The speech therapist, therefore, has an important role in educating staff about how dementia affects communication *and* how communication disorder does not necessarily signify dementia or confusion.

Staff will need to be taught how to adapt their communication skills to the individual case, whether a disorder is due to dementia, CVA or another cause. Lubinski suggests pairing communicatively impaired residents and staff members, to provide at least one communication partner for that person.

The provision of speech therapy services

It is still not usual for speech therapy services to be available within old peoples' homes, which has resulted in staff and residents being left to cope alone, or in occasional patients being transported to the speech therapy clinic, thus suffering the vagaries of weather and transport. For example, in the United States, Chapey *et al.* (1979) found that of the 25 per cent of homes that replied to their questionnaire three per cent had a speech therapist, and 27 per cent had part-time cover. Of all the homes, 21 per cent screened all residents for communication difficulty, while the rest relied upon referral in need.

Even if a post is approved there are still many difficulties in establishing a service within old peoples' homes. Funding for equipment may be difficult, particularly as such a post crosses the health and social services barrier. There is often a lack of space in the home, and a lack of time. The understanding of the speech therapist's role in homes is poor, not only among staff, but among the general public and other health professionals. Perhaps the greatest problem of all, however, is in motivating staff, who are often too busy, or uninterested, to attend. The following discussion may offer an optimistic view of obtaining the support of staff, but in reality this can be a time-consuming and depressing process. Unless the speech therapist has a strong conviction that his or her aims are critical to the quality of life of the institutionalised elderly person, little progress will be made. It must be stressed, however, that additional problems will arise if the therapist does not take time to learn about the home, plan goals carefully, and consider the practical difficulties faced by staff, before attempting to implement change.

INDIRECT WORK IN RESIDENTIAL HOMES

Education and attitude change

The initial step for the speech therapist working in an institutional setting, must be to educate, and thus attempt to change attitudes in the staff in such establishments. This will be covered in greater depth in the following chapter, but any staff-training programme will need a strong, articulate rationale, with a plan that is suitable for the particular environment in which it is to operate (Lubinski, 1984). There will be political difficulties in organising in-service training around staff levels and shifts, and frequently staff interest is low, perhaps as a result of the lack of recognition they receive for what is often soul-destroying work. Interest can only be gained if those who are committed to working with elderly people are aware of this need to inform and educate. A suitable training programme can have great benefits for the staff, in terms of job satisfaction, and vicariously for the residents. It is important that the speech therapist, or other outside professional, does not rush in too quickly, and wonder why staff are antagonistic. No changes will be maintained unless solid groundwork is done to obtain at least the co-operation, and it is hoped, the support of staff. Changes must stem from administrators and staff, and in order for them to be motivated they must understand the principles of a 'quality communication environment'.

Altering the physical environment

From the basis of a better-informed staff group, attempts can be made first to evaluate then to discuss and decide changes necessary in the physical environment. Lubinski suggests, wisely, beginning with a 'demonstration area' which should be carefully selected as having the potential for change, by virtue of the staff involved and the setting. Once those staff understand how the environment can influence communication, one can begin to focus on specific environmental factors.

Layout

Numerous researchers have commented on the effect layout of furniture can have on social interaction. Sommer and Ross (1958), for example, found more interaction between patients when chairs were moved into four person groupings, rather than left placed round the walls, as so often happens. Woods and Britton (1985) discussed the need for environmental modification in institutions, and point out some of the difficulties in maintaining any alterations such as failure to explain the reasons for them to *all* staff, including domestics and administrators.

Rearrangement of the traditional day room, to avoid the chairs lining the walls with residents side by side, and often further isolated by the wings of the typical 'geriatric chairs', should be a priority. Marston and Gupta (1977) suggests room

THE INSTITUTIONAL ENVIRONMENT

dividers, which would enclose circles of chairs, and which would help to avoid the tendency of both staff and residents to replace the chairs against the walls.

Other physical layout changes may be summed by, in Woods and Britton's phrase, 'a prosthetic environment' which would include memory aids, stable furniture, non-slip floors and so on. Whatever needs to be changed, goals should be formulated which are clear and attainable. Then when these are achieved all concerned will feel more motivated to embark on the next stage.

Lighting

Perhaps the most difficult problem in designing centres for an elderly population is in determining suitable levels of illumination. Fozard *et al.* (1977) point out that older people are more susceptible to glare, so a straightforward increase in illumination is not necessarily the answer. Allied to this is the increased likelihood that the older person will suffer from multiple visual problems, and this makes glasses hard to prescribe. Lighting should be at a level that helps to compensate for decreased visual acuity, and is also sufficient to allow residents to lip-read, to compensate for auditory impairment. One solution may be to allow more individual control of lighting, with extra lamps available for residents to use when necessary.

Acoustics

Although realistically in an institution a certain level of background noise is inevitable, efforts should be made to have quiet rooms available, and to keep the general noise level as low as possible. Hearing aid users will find adjustment particularly hard if background noise is high. The main barrier to quietness seems to be the indiscriminate turning on of radio and television, and it should be explained to staff that such background noise is a constant barrier to communication between residents and staff. Provision of daily newspapers or the television programme schedules will help more selective viewing; or when possible, a separate viewing room for residents who wish to watch television.

Privacy

The open, often noisy, lounge is not conductive to any

communication beyond immediate needs and social exchanges. Few will attempt more intimate or confidential conversations when there is a knowledge that others will overhear, and even gossip is restricted if the subject is in the same room! Kellaher *et al.* (1985) found that 75 per cent of their subjects had few friends of any depth, and that single room occupiers actually made more friends, perhaps, the authors suggest, indicating the value of having some private space. They found that whereas 90 per cent of their subjects, in state-run old peoples' homes in England would have chosen a single room, over 50 per cent were forced to share. Obviously, the numbers of rooms and of residents will not magically adjust, but the provision of quiet rooms which are separate from the lounge areas may allow a choice of privacy at times.

COMMUNICATION GROUPS

The speech therapist may be involved in planning and running group activities, in order to stimulate communication as a primary or secondary result of the group's aims. Such groups also provide an additional activity in what tends to be an unchanging routine, and provide subject matter for conversation outside the group. They can also demonstrate to residents that they are not uniquely 'sane in a mad world', but there are like-minded people in their home; and social periods within the group, perhaps providing tea or coffee, can emphasise this. It is worth noting that more homes are adopting unit-living schemes, in which smaller groups within the institution are run autonomously with their own living and dining areas, along broadly 'domestic' lines. These groupings can have the same benefits as the more artificial activity groups. Group members become 'givers' as well as 'takers', and are able to share and teach others as a result of their individual interests and experiences.

There are various 'types' of groups that can be used to stimulate communication, ranging from open discussion groups for mentally able residents, to more specialised groups with very particular aims, such as Reality Orientation. As speech therapists are frequently involved in Reality Orientation (RO) and Reminiscence groups, these will be specifically discussed; however, certain principles of group work will be generally applicable.

121

THE INSTITUTIONAL ENVIRONMENT

Planning

The most time consuming and crucial part of group work should be the planning period, prior to the first meeting. The first need is, of course, to establish the purposes and aims for that particular group. These will, to a great extent, determine the criteria for membership, the frequency of meeting, the activities and other practicalities. At the planning stage it is important to consider how the group will be evaluated, as often the easiest method is to administer pre- and post-group assessments, which enable staff to see if changes have occurred and aims been met. To a large extent careful evaluation will avoid the risk of groups becoming purposeless, and 'dragging on', without the results necessary to inspire continued enthusiasm and interest from both staff and members.

An evaluation may look at whether specific aims have been met, and/or assess general functioning of the members, for example, in terms of behavioural changes, communication and social interactions, and independence. It need not be complex — an example of a simple rating scale is given in the appendix, but it will be useful to gather views of the staff and of residents. If it transpires that the group was worthwhile a further course can be planned, incorporating any changes felt to be useful.

Members and staff

Participation should be a choice, although the apathy of home life does appear to justify gentle persuasion of residents at least to attend a group once. Careful selection of which residents to involve will greatly influence enjoyment of the group, and it is best to match psychological state and functional ability. If these are at a low level the group will need to be smaller. At least one member of staff from within the institution should be involved, but one interested person will be more valuable than numbers of co-opted 'helpers'. Problems of shifts will need to be sorted out during planning stages, not each time the group meets.

When and where

A quiet room will be needed, preferably one which can be used for every meeting as consistency is important, particularly for members who are confused. Distractions should be limited, and it should be ensured that, although near lavatory facilities, it is not the main thoroughfare for other residents! If the room is too large or too small, it will tend to distract members' attention,

122

and furniture should be comfortable and homely whenever possible.

Timetable clashes can be a problem and the possibility of this should be investigated at the planning stage. It is crucial particularly again for those members who are confused, that the group meets at a consistent time — which also allows staff not to risk being distracted by other tasks. The length of the course, and the frequency of meeting, will be pre-planned depending upon the aims of the group. It is important to arrange when the group will stop meeting, and not to continue unless it is fulfilling a purpose. When the course does end, perhaps after eight or ten sessions, any benefits can be assessed; and depending on the evaluation the group continued or not.

No group will work if staff are not made aware of, and involved in determining, its aims and purposes, or do not appreciate the value of its aims. Fitting the time, location and activities to the staff is as important as fitting them to the residents. The activities will largely depend on the aims, and two types of group will be used to demonstrate this point.

Reminiscence therapy

Reminiscing, in the therapeutic sense, may be viewed as the recall of past experience in order to adapt more satisfactorily to the present. Various types of reminiscing exist — life review, simple reminiscence, informative reminiscence, and positive reminiscence — which may prove to be particularly useful to particular client groups, but usually the term reminiscence is used to apply to a unitary phenomenon.

The main stimulus to use of reminiscence as therapy was found in the work of Erikson (1968), who saw the life cycle in stages. The final stage of life being to accept one's own past life as inevitable, and thus achieve 'integrity'. Butler (1963) also stressed the need for reminiscing, to help achieve this sense of acceptance of oneself, and readiness thus to face death. Talking about the past also serves a social function, and may help to preserve the individual's feelings of self worth. However, as Fallot (1979–80) points out, evidence is uncertain as to whether reminiscing leads older people to be better adjusted.

In therapeutic terms, the aims of reminiscence are to help maintain or improve the person's quality of life, and to cope better with the problems of old age (Norris and Eileh, 1982). It provides a structure within which an individual can be seen as an individual, rather than as an age or diagnostic label. Groups can, it is claimed, increase interaction and improve inter-resident relationships, by allowing sharing and identification of common interests (Norris and Eileh, 1982). However, the value of reminiscence is controversial; some have found links with lessened depression in members (Fallot, 1979–80; McMahon and Rhudick, 1964; and others), and with improved cognitive functioning (Hughston and Merriam 1982), but these may be the effects of treatment *per se*, not of reminiscence, and other studies have failed to find these links (e.g. Perrotta and Meacham, 1981–82).

Such contradictory findings suggest that the selection of members is very important. Despite anecdotal support, there is no real empirical evidence that reminiscence has a therapeutic value for dementia patients. However, the consensus seems to be that short-term benefits can be gained with depressed and low self-esteem patients. In institutions often the opportunity to reminisce is denied, through lack of partners or of privacy, for example, or as a result of confusion, sensory losses and ill health. An organised group can be used as a way of circumventing these obstacles.

The group activities must be pre-planned, partly to allow reminiscence aids to be gathered for use, such as photographs, old objects, slides or tapes. These aids should aim to appeal to all senses, in order to stimulate memories by taste, touch and smell, as well as sight and hearing. The former senses can be potent stimuli for recall.

As in any group, all contributions must be treated as worthwhile, and staff should emphasise what members *can* do, not what they cannot do. Perhaps more than in other types of groups it is important in reminiscence work to remember the possible age differences between the members.

Reality orientation

Reality orientation, or RO, was first used in the United States in 1958, and has become a frequent form of group therapy in most western societies. It is designed for use with confused and dementing patients, and aims to orient them to their environment by constant repetition. It may take the form of formal 'classroom' sessions, but more importantly acts as an informal or '24 hour' philosophy of care, by which staff are encouraged to speak to patients as often as possible, continually reminding them of who and where they are, the time and what is happening.

Formal or Group RO supplements this 24 hour approach to care. Groups must meet at a consistent time and place, and may cater for basic, standard or advanced levels, depending on the abilities of members. It is, perhaps, a shame that RO had such massive claims made for it by early proponents. There is, for example, no evidence that it can 'reawaken unused neurological pathways'. Clinically, however, it has many supporters who feel that it can help 'sociability, co-operation and self-pride' (Powell-Proctor, 1980). Empirical evidence suggests that any improvements are directly linked to the content of the programme, and does not conclusively suggest that they generalise or persist following the cessation of group work. RO does seem to be beneficial in that it stimulates staff interest, and can lead to attitude change and a less 'institutionalised' approach to care. In this particular way its effect may be greater than other group work, because it is not limited to the formal group setting.

As with all groups, realistic goals must be set, members carefully matched, and programmes pre-planned. An eight session RO programme might, for example, at a basic level, stress only name, place and time. An advanced group may include the weather and season, meals, news and local matters. Each subject can be repeated using different methods of media; 'names' for example, may involve self-introductions, making name cards or badges, selecting one's own name from a list, matching other members to names, taking and matching photographs to people and names and so on. A useful manual on RO has been compiled by Rimmer (1982) who also suggests how such groups may be evaluated.

Thus the speech therapist will have a role in working with older people in residential settings, not only with those who have specific communication disorders, but indirectly with all residents, with the aim of removing obstacles to successful and enjoyable communication and thus improving their quality of life.

THE INSTITUTIONAL ENVIRONMENT

APPENDIX 7.1: COMMUNICATION ENVIRONMENT

Circle the appropriate number where you feel the frequency of occurrence is represented (e.g. centrally if it occurs sometimes).

	1 Frequently/ Much	2 3 4	5 Never/ Little

A. OPPORTUNITIES

1. Does the individual take part in an activity, of his choice, that stimulates conversation?

Daily	1	2 3 4	5
Weekly	1	2 3 4	5

2. Do people around encourage interesting activities?

Family	1	2 3 4	5
Spouse	1	2 3 4	5
Medical staff	1	2 3 4	5
Roommate	1	2 3 4	5
Friends	1	2 3 4	5
Others			

3. Does s/he have a variety of social contacts?

Work	1	2 3 4	5
Leisure	1	2 3 4	5
Religion	1	2 3 4	5
Friendship	1	2 3 4	5
Home life	1	2 3 4	5
Other			

4. Is there frequent opportunity to communicate with:

Family	1	2 3 4	5
Medical/care staff	1	2 3 4	5
Roommate	1	2 3 4	5
Friends	1	2 3 4	5

5. Does s/he have at least one person with whom to communicate personal thoughts?

If so, name the person/ relationship	1	2 3 4	5

6. Is s/he encouraged to talk about a variety of topics?

Personal information	1	2 3 4	5
Objects	1	2 3 4	5
People	1	2 3 4	5
Relationships	1	2 3 4	5

THE INSTITUTIONAL ENVIRONMENT

	1 Frequently/ Much	2 3 4	5 Never/ Little
Abstract ideas	1	2 3 4	5
Social amenities	1	2 3 4	5
News	1	2 3 4	5
Other	1	2 3 4	5

7. Is s/he encouraged to use a variety of communication methods?

Talking	1	2 3 4	5
Writing	1	2 3 4	5
Gesturing	1	2 3 4	5
Communication aid	1	2 3 4	5
Other	1	2 3 4	5

8. Is counselling available to the family?

In hospital	1	2 3 4	5
At home	1	2 3 4	5
In support group	1	2 3 4	5

9. Does the physical environment provide a variety of:

Colours	1	2 3 4	5
Sounds	1	2 3 4	5
Smells	1	2 3 4	5
Textures	1	2 3 4	5
Actions	1	2 3 4	5

B. BARRIERS

1. Do people know about the communication impairment?

Family	1	2 3 4	5
Staff	1	2 3 4	5
Friends	1	2 3 4	5
Others	1	2 3 4	5

2. Do you understand *how* to speak to the individual?

Family	1	2 3 4	5
Staff	1	2 3 4	5
Friends	1	2 3 4	5
Others	1	2 3 4	5

3. Do people check for signs of comprehension?

Family	1	2 3 4	5
Staff	1	2 3 4	5
Friends	1	2 3 4	5
Others	1	2 3 4	5

THE INSTITUTIONAL ENVIRONMENT

	1 Frequently/ Much	2	3	4	5 Never/ Little
4 Do people pressure the individual to talk, or complete sentences for them?					
Family	1	2	3	4	5
Staff	1	2	3	4	5
Friends	1	2	3	4	5
Others	1	2	3	4	5
5. Do people avoid involving the individual in conversation?					
Family	1	2	3	4	5
Staff	1	2	3	4	5
Friends	1	2	3	4	5
Others	1	2	3	4	5
6. Do people limit the topics they are prepared to introduce?					
Family	1	2	3	4	5
Staff	1	2	3	4	5
Friends	1	2	3	4	5
Others	1	2	3	4	5

APPENDIX 7.2: GROUP EVALUATION

Name:　　　　*Date of birth*　　　　*Date:*

pre- post- group (circle appropriate)

		Good 5	4	3	2	*Poor/* *Absent* 1
Orientation	– person					
	– place					
	– time					
Concentration						
Interaction	– with family					
	– with staff					
	– with other residents					
Memory						
Independence	– dressing					
	– washing					
	– eating					
Communication	– starting conversations					
	– listening to others					
	– maintaining conversations					

In your opinion has the group helped this person?

8

The Multidisciplinary Team

In 1975 Leutenegger wrote 'none of us, as rehabilitation specialists, can function autonomously . . . not only must the staff discuss the patients' needs and attitudes, but they need also to talk with the patient about what and how he is doing . . . Other members of the staff, as well as family members, need to see the full array of the patients' problems.'

He is, of course, describing the multidisciplinary team approach, about which so much has been said over the last ten years. While this approach has been adopted in many fields of medicine — with varying degrees of success — it is perhaps most relevant in geriatric and psychogeriatric care which overlap with so many other disciplines in both health and social services. There are difficulties in any field in establishing a working team, some of which will be discussed later in this chapter, but a very real and specific problem in working with an elderly population is in the attitudes held by so many health and social service professionals towards this patient group.

ATTITUDES TO 'THE ELDERLY'

The term 'ageism' has entered the English vocabulary over the last few years, to describe the 'systemic stereotyping of people and discrimination against them on the basis of age' (Beverly, 1975). These attitudes are not found only in the young, but are held by many elderly people, and until individuals recognise that their own beliefs and opinions should change, there will be little headway made in accepting older members of our society as having an important part to play. However, it does appear

129

that exposure to information can alter the way in which individuals view 'the aged'.

There is, of course, some basis for the stereotyped picture of older people, as was seen in Chapter 1, in that they do face greater risks of suffering mental or physical disorder. However, as was indicated then, it is a minority of older people who place the exaggerated demand on the services which is generalised to all over 65-year-olds. As Freer (1985) points out, there is a need for the 'widespread negative image of old age', to be corrected, and this must stem from attitude change not only in the young. The older person who accepts a lower standard of performance as an inevitable part of old age, and therefore fails to report illness to the doctor, for example, must also change.

Health and social service employees working with elderly people also tend to hold a negative stereotype of them, and this becomes a barrier to successful communication, as it disrupts what Shadden, Raiford and Shadden (1983) describe as the 'communicative balance' of an interaction. Most professions still fail to train their members sufficiently in aspects of aging and related management principles, particularly in the sense of providing an overall view, and covering other disciplines' involvement as well as their own. Few professions, for example, are informed on the process of aging in relation to communication.

Weiss (1971) talked specifically about attitudes towards the communicative needs of older people. He felt that generalisations included the feeling that they need fewer communication skills, because they exist within a restricted environment and they lack interest in communication, and that elderly people themselves are negative about rehabilitation. Weiss sums up by saying 'I doubt that these assumptions foster objective and enthusiastic interest in communication of the aged, or that they are entirely justified'.

This chapter will discuss the role of the speech therapist within the multidisciplinary team, and the need for the therapist to be involved in teaching other team members about the communication process and aging.

THE MULTIDISCIPLINARY TEAM

Leutenegger's comments, at the beginning of this chapter,

outline the reasons behind the team approach to patient care—namely, the need for all involved with any one patient to know how other professions (and the patient) view his needs, and how they are working towards them. This presupposes good communication between team members, and, while a leader is necessary in the sense of chairing the discussions and co-ordinating efforts, a democratic rather than authoritarian approach to decision making. In the past, the latter was the norm, and it is sadly still seen on many occasions, with certain professions being seen as having less of value to contribute. It is hoped that the trend is swinging towards a more democratic approach.

The way in which individual team members view their own roles will be an important factor in whether the team works as such, rather than as a group of individuals. Some see their role as being to apply their own specialised skills, and then to report back to other members of the team — an approach which may be described as 'territorial'. Others adopt a 'permissive' approach, seeing themselves as 'cutting across disciplinary lines', through remotivation and resocialisation' (Eisdorfer and Stotsky, 1977). There is no compelling evidence that either is better than the other, but a combination of the two seems to provide the most cohesive team, and thus the most effective and comprehensive patient care.

Jacques, speaking in Edinburgh in 1985, described each professional as having a pool of knowledge, as a result of training and experience, some of which could be seen as essential to his or her present position. While both the background knowledge and essential skills will in part overlap with other disciplines (some may share many abilities, such as Psychiatry and Clinical Psychology; others fewer, such as Nursing and Speech Therapy) each will retain certain abilities and functions which are specific to themselves — for example, only the medical staff are able to prescribe drugs, only the speech therapist will be expected to implement programmes specifically aiming to improve speech and language skills, and so on.

Gray (1982), in a brief article, made this same point, that 'unity does not preclude autonomy', and the acknowledgement of different points of view is a part of successful teamwork. Similarly, there is no one way for a team to function; this will stem not just from the different professions involved, but from

The team in the hospital

It is the norm for teams to operate under the leadership of the consultant in that particular medical discipline. Thus, some professionals will be members of only one such team, nursing staff for example, while others, like speech therapists, will have patients to be discussed in various different fields — perhaps in neurology, ENT and geriatrics, for example.

The aims of hospital care of elderly people have been described by Isaacs (1977) as 'the undertaking of active investigation and rehabilitation using the services of an integrated multidisciplinary team, and with the object of early planned discharge and continuing community supervision'. Basically, the team approach should ensure that comprehensive care is offered to allow maximal functional ability in each patient. The attitude of the team towards the elderly person will be a critical factor in how well their aims are met, and how far beyond this direct role the team extends. Many feel, for example, some responsibility towards changing the attitudes of others by helping them to recognise the heterogeneity of the elderly population as a 'medical consumer group'.

The hospital-based team has the advantage of a single geographical location. Thus regular meetings are easier to organise than they would be in the more dispersed community setting, although problems may still arise for those professions who overlap various medical specialisations, or who may only occasionally see patients cared for by a particular team. Speech and language clinicians often have to face these difficulties, and regular, rather than frequent, attendance at meetings may be the answer. This at least enables structured links to be maintained, and allows for discussion of specific patients or for a more general consultative role.

One difficulty that can occur within the hospital setting is that of maintaining good links between teams, not just within teams. At times the patient risks becoming a statistic, or bargaining pawn, to be played off for economic organisational reasons.

The team in the community

Adopting a team approach within the community is fraught with practical problems. While hospital teams are discussing a specific geographical group, patients in the community are widely dispersed, and will often not share the same permutation of services in their care programmes. By definition, their care will be less acute, and aims will differ, often being maintenance rather than rehabilitation. Similarly, there will be patients who only need to receive input from one particular discipline — be it for speech therapy, drug therapy or any other service.

However, many individuals would benefit if a more integrated team approach were possible within the community. This is becoming more of a dilemma, and often a stumbling block, as more elderly people are returned to the community to be maintained by the provision of varied services. Team discussion may indicate that additional services are needed, not only for the patient, but in order to support families and other carers, who are expected to take the burden of care upon themselves when individuals are discharged from hospital.

The 'leadership' question is rarely asked in hospital care, as it falls to the medical staff and thus to their internal hierarchy, and it tends, rightly or wrongly, to be their decision as to whether a democratic or authoritarian mode is adopted. However, in the community the question of who leads or convenes meetings is a thorny one. Many would automatically see the family doctor in this light, but this may not be the best choice, either in terms of time available, or indeed motivation to perform the role. Fox (1985) makes the point that family doctors all too often see the management of chronic illness as secondary to the curing role, yet it is in the former case when the team can often contribute most. This is markedly demonstrated in the care of dementing patients. Murphy (1985) suggests that over 80 per cent of dementia sufferers are unknown to their family doctor, and that it is rare for that doctor to alert other services when cases are presented, either in terms of hospital investigations or community support systems. Strang, Caine and Acheson (1983) described team care of elderly patients, from a general practice viewpoint, and found that many of the primary care workers were sceptical, and only lip service was paid to the idea. They stress the need

THE MULTIDISCIPLINARY TEAM

for the team to be 'a whole that is greater than the sum of its parts'.

The team in the community may be best served by adopting a case work approach towards those patients who present management problems. A 'key worker' would then be responsible for organising the meeting, in much the same way as the cases of children at risk are discussed. It must then be agreed upon as to who does what, and followed up by effective intervention. Each community worker must be aware of the role of other disciplines, and be prepared to contact them for advice and support, and to inform others of their own involvement. Sadly at present the experiences of many workers lead them to see the team approach in the community as only an ideal.

Who's who in the team

Ultimately, whether hospital or community based, the team will work if the individual personalities in it gel, and each individual recognises the importance of every member of the team. This should include not only the recognised health and social service professionals, but also other caring workers who are all too often neglected, but who are much more relevant often to the daily functioning of individual patients. Among such would be included the lay-carers — family or friends — and any voluntary bodies involved on a regular basis, and, for example, non-professional groups, such as the grossly under-rated home help/ domestic care service. Most importantly, perhaps, the team should be seen to include the patient, for it is his or her life which will be affected by the decisions made by the team.

Many disciplines may be involved in caring for the older person in hospital and community; and there will obviously be overlap, most notably when community patients continue to attend out-patient clinics, or when hospital staff are asked to undertake domiciliary visits. There are also many 'fringe' professions involved in working with older people for which funding is rarely available, such as music, art and drama therapists.

It is worth reiterating at this point that there is a great need for those professionals working with an aged population to have their roles recognised by the other medical disciplines, and to

134

feel their worth is appreciated. At present, all too often 'geriatrics' is seen as the bottom of the barrel, and it is not surprising that few choose this field as the preferred area of expertise. Perhaps those already in the field should also recognise the need that Martin (1983) stresses 'for more enthusiasm in health professionals based on the patient *not* his age'.

Volunteers

One possible member of the team who has not been mentioned, and whose role is far from clearly defined, is the volunteer worker. Many speech therapists use volunteers to work with communicatively disordered people of all ages, and various volunteer schemes have been discussed in the literature. The most quoted of such schemes have been those designed to assess the efficacy of speech therapy with adult aphasic patients.

Such debates should not draw attention away from the fact that volunteers may have a valuable role to play in rehabilitating aphasic and other communicatively impaired people. Whether this role is most valuable in terms of social stimulation and increasing social confidence, as seems to have been the case in the Speech-after-Stroke Scheme described by Eaton-Griffiths (1975), or whether they can be used to attempt to improve specific language skills is in one sense academic if the patient at the end of the day is more able to function in his daily life.

Volunteers usually undergo some degree of training and work under the supervision of qualified speech therapists. As with any organisation or group, individual experience and knowledge will differ, but it is important to ensure that volunteers have a basic understanding of the nature of aphasia, dysarthria, dementia or any other disorder with which they will come into contact. Input from allied professions in the training can be of great value.

THE SPEECH THERAPIST AS A TEAM MEMBER

It is interesting to ask other professionals how they would view the role of the speech therapist in the care of elderly; or of psychogeriatric, patients. Often this will differ markedly from the speech therapist's own perceptions, and unless the therapist is convinced of her role it will be impossible to ensure that others understand. This is not difficult in working directly with speech or language handicapped patients, but presents problems for some therapists beginning to take on more indirect functions. Gray (1982) points out the 'fundamental need to know what we are doing and *why*' and that therapists must be prepared to communicate this to patient, family and professionals, without recourse to incomprehensible professional jargon.

The medical model — direct curative work with the patient — may not be the most appropriate or useful use of time in the field of geriatrics perhaps more than in any other. The speech therapist will often face working within a team where members have little knowledge of communication, and even less of how this relates to older people. Thus an educational role is forced upon the therapist, and this will be discussed at some length in this chapter. The reasons for this are several, but largely stem from the fact that, while expected to teach various groups about speech therapy, little attention has been given to teaching the speech therapist how best to convey this information. The ultimate aim of teaching is to change attitudes towards older people and how they communicate; but specifically the therapist must be prepared to teach about particular problems and patients, when this is relevant to the team.

As a team member, the speech therapist must be able to contribute and, when necessary, to argue for patient care to follow a particular course, and not just report her own 'solo' assessment findings and therapy methods. Being a fully integrated team member should, as Gray says, not diminish the role of the speech therapist, but should 'clarify the particular skills (she) has to offer'.

The teaching role

The aims and methods of teaching must differ, depending on the audience. Shadden *et al.* (1983) suggest that the speech therapist should consider 'members of any health profession or organisation involved in service delivery to the older population' as potential target audiences. It is thus important not to restrict the teaching role to other health professions. Certain key organisations could be viewed as a priority in terms of their need to know about communication with elderly people and they are those who either have regular, frequent contact with

136

the elderly population, such as care staff in residential homes, home helps, and families; or those who are in a position to pick up speech or language disorders and refer them to the speech therapist (such as the family doctor).

There are numerous practical considerations in planning a teaching session or course, and it is important for these details to be settled as early as possible. Obviously, if invited by other disciplines or groups, these will largely be avoided, but if the course is self-instigated, decisions must be made regarding the target audience, the site, dates, equipment and teaching method, and funding. Most importantly, once the audience is selected, is the need to plan the content in order for the session to be relevant to that population.

Target population and size of audience

It is probably wise not to attempt to mix different professional groups, unless they are linked in their specific area of specialisation, or to mix professional and lay populations. The presenter can then concentrate only on the aspects which are relevant to the whole audience, and approach them at an appropriate level. The size of the audience will depend on such factors as room size, and preferred teaching method, and it is important that these considerations are not forgotten.

Site

A suitable location must be booked to allow the audience easy access. If the invited audience includes disabled people, for example, suitable facilities must be available, and it will be more important that the location is on good bus or rail routes. Again, the teaching method will be a factor, as a formal lecture theatre will make audience participation difficult.

Timing

The amount of information to be conveyed and the time available to audience and presenter(s) will determine whether a single session, be it one hour or a whole day, or a course of lectures is most appropriate. If the latter is decided, it is usually best not to leave too long between sessions. If the audience is scattered, it may be useful to assess interest and timing preferences, by distributing a questionnaire prior to planning the course in detail.

Teaching style and methods

The nature of the audience will determine the most appropriate teaching style in many instances. Some professions or organisations will not be used to a formal lecture format, and will find it difficult to learn in this way. Shadden *et al.* (1983) suggest a mixture of styles to maintain interest. They use lectures supplemented by visual aids and handouts; the latter can be most useful as they reinforce what is said, and can be digested by those attending in their own time. Some examples of general advice sheets used with relatives, nursing and other groups are given in the appendix to this chapter (p. 140).

'Audience participation' tasks may be used to develop a more realistic understanding of the nature of communication, and of possible disorders. Discussion allows participants to explore their own attitudes and reactions, and to clarify any misapprehensions, although there is the danger that one or two people will monopolise discussion time. Visual aids, such as slides or overheads, are extremely useful to keep the attention of the audience and to illustrate points made in the talk.

Funding

Often the question of funding in a direct sense is irrelevant, if talks are internal within a hospital or district. If, however, funds are needed in order to book rooms or equipment, or to pay outside lecturers, it is often possible to charge participants. Some groups may see this as a barrier, and it may then be possible to obtain sponsorship to pay all or part of the costs, or perhaps to provide refreshments. If the lecture centres on a particular disorder, this will be easier to obtain, perhaps from relevant drug companies or charities.

Content — what do they need to know?

It is important that the nature of the audience is considered, rather than the same information being offered to all disciplines or organisations. To illustrate this point, three groups will be briefly considered — the home help service, residential care staff and general practitioners/family doctors.

The home help service is often the most frequent contact for an older person living at home. In an unpublished study at Charing Cross Hospital, London (Moon, 1984), home help organisers felt on average 35 per cent of their elderly clients faced some degree of communication difficulty, with deafness being the major handicap. The medical reasons and statistics for the difficulties were not of great interest to these organisers, but their perceived need was for home helps to know how to talk to such clients. Thus the content of a course or talk would need to be very practical and could, for example, make use of the handouts suggested in the appendix to this chapter (p 140).

Residential care staff are, by definition, working with a more handicapped section of the elderly population, some of whom will have communication difficulties. Their role has been discussed more fully in Chapter 7. Their needs in terms of education about communication have been discussed by Lubinski (1981b), who suggested a series of in-service training sessions covering, among other things, a consideration of how the institutional environment affects communication, and the value of communication.

Family doctors, on the other hand, have no need to learn of institutional effects on communication, although they should be aware that they exist, and as they tend to see patients infrequently, they also have less need (or less perceived need) to be told how to talk to specific patients. However, they are often in the best position to pick up and refer communicatively impaired people, and therefore it may be most useful to plan to offer information about services available, how to refer and who to refer. If there is interest in more detailed consideration of the various disorders, this might be suitable as a follow-up lecture.

These examples are not intended as evidencing the only way to approach these groups, nor as covering all the necessary information, but merely to indicate the need to consider what information is relevant to the different disciplines, outside the specific discussion of a particular client. In most instances, it will be useful, even when intending to cover specific disorders, to teach first about the normal communication process and the effect of aging upon it. This will provide a framework into which the disorders can be fitted, and thus better understood in terms of their effect upon individual sufferers.

Evaluation

Whenever possible, it is important to attempt to measure the value of teaching programmes, in order to know whether to repeat such courses, to amend them, or to reject them. This may be done by assessing attitudes, knowledge or behaviours

THE MULTIDISCIPLINARY TEAM

before and after the course, either by interview, questionnaire or observation, to assess whether changes have occurred.

Evaluation of individual sessions or speakers within the course can also be carried out in these ways, or by using rating scales. Shadden *et al.* (1983) suggest rating participants' views on content, whether objectives were met, use of information, and interest level, among other aspects of an education programme. Obviously, the most detailed evaluation will be pointless unless the results are carefully studied and action is taken in response to them. Failure to evaluate may well mean considerable time is being spent on far from useful teaching sessions. If evaluation is carried out, and taken account of, then the speech therapist may find time spent in teaching about elderly people and communication is rewarding both in personal terms and in the more important terms of patient care.

Thus, the speech therapist can play a role in the team approach to patient care, in offering advice and comments on the management of individual patients that come before the team, and in offering general advice on the nature of communication difficulties in an elderly population. As a team member, however, the therapist must also be prepared to listen to the opinions of others on individual patients, and to learn from them about their varied roles in caring for elderly people. The multidisciplinary team can only work if each person within it is prepared to respect the contributions of the rest of the team as being as relevant and valuable as his or her own contribution, while not losing sight of their individual area of expertise and skill.

APPENDIX 8

(a) *Talking to . . . elderly people*
    (1) Above all, treat them as intelligent individuals — they may alter as they get older in many ways but are not less adult. Do *not* treat them or talk to them as children!
    (2) Check they are wearing hearing aids/glasses, teeth etc. (or if necessary refer them to the appropriate professional).
    (3) Allow them *TIME* — to get to know you; to understand what is going on; to follow conversation and to reply; to accept new faces and general change.
    (4) Don't assume their interests — give them the choice to participate and the opportunity to direct the conversation as you would any adult.

THE MULTIDISCIPLINARY TEAM

(5) Repeat new information as often as necessary — they are not stupid but they may need more time to adjust.
(6) Don't change the subject quickly and unexpectedly.
(7) Don't spend too long, especially if you are asking them to concentrate.
(8) If you are not sure that they have understood it may help to speak more slowly or demonstrate what you want them to do; or ask them to repeat what they understood you to mean.
(9) Remember people vary in how they age — some 90-year-olds are just as quick-witted as you are, and would like to be treated as such!
(10) Allow them to talk about how they feel without judging them, or dismissing what they say as worthless. It may seem trivial or hard for you to appreciate, but is very real to them.
(11) Especially allow them to express how they feel about death, without trying to 'jolly' them along unrealistically.
(12) *'Adjust to the individual NOT the age'.*

(b) *Talking to . . . the person with intellectual or memory impairment*
(1) Establish a simple and consistent routine and environment (for example, do not move objects from their familiar place).
(2) Minimise distractions.
(3) Frequent reminders of time, place and person are often necessary to keep the conversation going. Always use their name, and 'talk through' daily events ('It's 12 o'clock, Rose, time for lunch').
(4) Display pictures of family and friends (and any others who have regular contact).
(5) Speech may seem rambling and 'odd'. Tact is needed to bring the conversation back to the subject — either by a question or gentle reminder.
(6) If the conversation is getting nowhere do not feel you must force the person to carry on. Come back to it after a break.
(7) They may deny the problem and blame others — avoid arguments, or trying to solve a disagreement. Instead change the subject.
(8) Use concrete and familiar terms and topics. Avoid sarcasm, anecdotes and complex explanations.
(9) Such individuals are at risk of being spoken to like children. Avoid doing this.
(10) You should always gain their attention before talking to them.
(11) Do not reward inappropriate language but encourage any attempt to communicate.
(12) Allow them to talk about the 'old days' which is often easier and clearer, but link it with the 'here and now' to orientate them to reality. ('It only cost a little when you were young — now it's . . .').

(c) *Talking to . . . the hard of hearing*
(1) Make sure the surroundings are as quiet as possible. Turn

141

THE MULTIDISCIPLINARY TEAM

down radios and TVs. Close doors and windows if noise outside is loud.

(2) Let the light fall on your face so the deaf or hard of hearing person can see your lips, facial expression and gesture. Avoid gestures and hand movements that cover your mouth. Do not speak while chewing or eating.

(3) Before speaking, gain attention by, for example, touching their shoulder. If in a chair, or wheelchair, bend or sit so that your faces are on the same level.

(4) Speak clearly and slowly, without over-exaggeration of mouth movements. Do *not* shout, but speak at a good, loud level. If you know which ear is better for the listener, speak to this side.

(5) Especially in a group, give the person a clue as to what you are talking about, and avoid sudden changes of subject.

(6) Avoid long, involved sentences. If you need to repeat, rephrase the sentence making it shorter and simpler if possible. Do not talk 'down' to them. Use signs or pointing to illustrate.

(7) If telling a complex story . . . every so often wait to check the person is following.

(8) Be conscious that people may try to cover up their hearing loss, and indicate your sympathy and willingness to help.

(d) *Talking to . . . the hearing aid wearer*

(1) Speak slowly and distinctly, but do not shout or raise your voice too much.

(2) Encourage the person always to wear the aid when you talk to them.

(3) Find out how the aid works so you can help the user if problems arise, such as battery changing or volume settings.

(4) Remember to speak 'to' the aid where amplification takes place — so, to the aid side if a behind-the-ear aid is worn, or from the front if a body worn aid is worn.

(5) Encourage prompt attendance at the clinic if the aid is not working.

(6) Encourage the user to have regular check-ups, as aids may need updating. The audiometrist will suggest how long to leave between checks.

(7) Continue to follow the advice suggested for talking to the hard of hearing.

(e) *Talking to . . . the aphasic*

(1) Talk in a quiet, relaxed atmosphere without distractions.

(2) Gain the person's attention before speaking — by touching or saying his name.

(3) Use facial expression and gesture to 'back up' your words.

(4) Speak somewhat more slowly, and keep your utterance short, simple and direct (but not childlike). Emphasise key words but do not raise your voice.

THE MULTIDISCIPLINARY TEAM

(5) Be prepared to repeat more often, but do not try to 'get through' by volume!

(6) Make questions simple and direct — those requiring yes/no answers are often the most useful.

(7) The aphasic may have difficulty selecting the word they want and in monitoring this. Ask questions to clarify what they intended to convey.

(8) Do not be surprised or upset if the person swears more than they used to. It may upset them too, so downplay this aspect.

(9) Do not 'correct' the errors, but encourage further responses, but do not pressurise them to respond.

(10) Remember their ability fluctuates — saying a word one day does not mean they will be able to the next day.

(11) Avoid vague, abstract subjects.

(12) Encourage all attempts at communicating whether by word, facial expression, or gesture.

(13) Avoid trying to talk for the person — you may put words into their mouth!

(14) Make every contact an opportunity for conversation, in order to provide stimulation and to give them something to want to chat about.

(15) An aphasic may well have visual or hearing problems. Make sure any aids (glasses or for hearing) are working and be prepared to ask for professional advice.

(16) Always ask the speech therapist for more specific explanations and advice about an individual.

(17) Never discuss the person in his or her presence as if they were not there; even if they appear to understand little they may grasp fragments or the tone of any conversation.

(f) *Talking to . . . the dysarthric*

(1) Do not pretend you understand if you don't. This will usually be obvious to the speaker and cause great frustration.

(2) Be patient and tolerant, as their speech will be slow and take great effort. Remind them that you will give them time to get their message across.

(3) Do not demand lengthy, complex responses, as this will tire the dysarthric. When tired, anyway, speech may well be less clear, and it is a good idea to 'try again' after a rest rather than persisting.

(4) Help by making the surroundings quiet. Face the speaker so you can watch his mouth and facial movements. Do not speak at the same time, or interrupt. You don't need to raise your voice unless there is a hearing problem as well.

(5) If the person is physically able to write, provide paper and pencil or pictures to point to (or use any aids that have been suggested) either to supplement or use instead of speech attempts. If at all possible, encourage speech efforts, but other methods can lessen frustration.

(6) Repeat the part of a message you can understand, so the

THE MULTIDISCIPLINARY TEAM

speaker does not have to go through it all again; or ask appropriate questions to establish clearly what is meant. Nodding or asking questions will show you are following what is said.

(7) Do not be afraid to ask for a message to be repeated. If necessary, ask for one word at a time, or for a particular word to be spelt out. Let them know the best rate for them to speak at, which you can understand.

(8) Specific advice may remind the person of the best way to adjust their speech — check with the speech therapist.

9

Families

One of the myths of the modern age is the persistent stereotyped image of huge numbers of aged people vegetating in institutions. It has already been commented upon that there is an overwhelming majority who live in the community, either alone or with relatives. Only five to six per cent of over 65-year-olds live in residential or hospital accommodation, and of the rest, about 34 per cent live alone, 52 per cent with a spouse, and 8 per cent with other people. While it is true that the Western system has, over recent years, stressed independence and encouraged older individuals to make use of services outside the family as and when necessary, and to continue living alone, it is also true that even those who do live alone are usually in regular contact with their relatives (Shanas *et al.*, 1968). The primary caregiver tends to be the spouse, or, in the case of widowed or unmarried elderly people, the closest female relative — most commonly a daughter or sister.

However, helping networks are not evenly spread, and there are considerable ethnic differences, and cultural variations. First generation migrants tend to retain their native land's philosophies in caring for their elderly relations, but second and third generation tend gradually to adopt the system of their 'new' homeland. Thus, they are more prepared to use the professional services available to them, including old people's homes.

However, the family remains the primary source of support for most older people, and recognition of this leads to appreciation of the fact not only that there are large numbers of elderly people in the community who need support; but many families who are accepting the burdens of the caring role, who are themselves in need of support. A communication disorder will affect not only the sufferer, but the whole family profoundly, and thus can be described as 'a family problem'.

THE EFFECTS OF COMMUNICATION DISORDERS ON THE FAMILY

Kinsella and Duffy (1978) found that the spouse of an aphasic was more likely to suffer from depression than that of a hemiplegic with intact language skills. Malone (1969) in a survey of twenty families who had an aphasic member found that the most frequent problems encountered were spouse role change, income reduction, reduced social opportunities and increased health problems. Family reactions to these include hostility, frustration, guilt, rejection and over-solicitousness. Artes and Hoops (1976) concluded from their work that aphasia is more of a social problem than other sequelae of stroke. Their subjects' wives were found to be more pessimistic, more self-pitying and more hypercritical in comparison to the wives of non-aphasic stroke victims. Despite these findings, only half the aphasics' wives interviewed perceived the communication problem to be the major adjustment difficulty.

The influence of other communication problems such as dysarthria, on the sufferers' families has not been studied. The intuitive feeling of many therapists is that severity must be a major factor, but as has been seen in other contexts, it is often not the objective reality that determines outcome, but the subjective perceptions of the 'protagonists'. This could be a valuable area of study, particularly if research is biased towards the clinical needs of the family in adjusting to a handicapped member.

There will, when the communicatively impaired individual is elderly, also be the effects of having an aged person within the family. The communication patterns within the household alter as individual members age. Retirement, and other age-related changes in life-style result in the older person's having fewer 'roles' and fewer interaction partners (Neugarten and Gutman, 1958). Thus, the other family members alter their perceptions of that older individual (partly as a result of the pervasive stereotyped view of 'the old'), and there are often subtle changes in the way in which interaction occurs. Family roles adapt in order to compliment those of the other family members.

Communication may adapt successfully, or there may be negative sequelae for both the older person and the family. If difficulties exist prior to onset of a specific speech or language disorder, they will be compounded and exaggerate the subsequent functional difficulties faced by patient and family. A further factor is the tendency of families to close ranks against 'outsiders'. While in some situations this is useful and supportive, in other cases covering up difficulties or lack of cohesion can only serve to increase the likelihood of a later crisis.

If the burden of caring becomes excessive it may be that the family are forced to consider whether the older person should be admitted to an old peoples' home or hospital. This is obviously a very distressing time for the elderly person, who may often perceive it as 'a move to die' (Gifford, 1980). However, the family will often also experience great emotional trauma as a result of making the decision, and professionals working with an older population must be sensitive to the problems on both sides.

In summary, poor adjustment to the aging process, and therefore to the 'aging' of communication skills, will affect the individual's whole family (Erikson, 1968). If a communication disorder is suffered, it will both exaggerate prior difficulties and as a result of its pervasive influence on daily living, create very great adjustment problems for members of the family. It seems crucial, then to consider how families can be helped to face these problems, and accept their new situation.

THE INFLUENCE OF THE FAMILY ON THE COMMUNICATIVELY DISORDERED MEMBER

As much as the communication disorder affects the family, so the family will affect the handicapped person, and their influence may be helpful or hindering. Mulhall (1978) looked at mutual influences, and found evidence that some problems of the spouse will affect the aphasic patient. Haspiel, Clement and Haspiel (1972) demonstrated that the speech or language handicapped person may become the scapegoat for other family difficulties. It would seem that age may also influence this negative reaction to any one family member.

Thus the family can be a major factor in whether an individual successfully adjusts both to the aging process and to a specific disorder. They will also play a critical part in rehabilitation — whether or not they are asked to take on a direct 'teaching' role. Schewan and Cameron (1984) stress this family influence when they state that the speech therapist may be able 'to facilitate the best communicative environment for the aphasic person through family counselling'. There is a great deal of anecdotal evidence for the positive and negative effect that the family may have on the rehabilitation process, but there has been little written which objectively considers how the therapist can best counsel that family to create the positive support which will facilitate rehabilitation work. There is little doubt that mis-timing of intervention with the family, or inappropriate content, will hinder rather than help, despite the best efforts of the therapist.

INTERVENTION WITH THE FAMILY

One goal of family intervention is to enable that family to adjust to and accept the communication handicap, and to achieve stability (Webster and Newhoff, 1981). The second major goal is to enable the family to support the patient's attempts at rehabilitation. In order to work towards these aims, the therapist will need to know a considerable amount about the way in which a particular family functions and interacts. Not all families appear to need outside support; some cope with minimal input. Others face enormous difficulties in adjusting, and there are those who fall into the 'no-man's land' between — appearing to cope, but having underlying problems which they are unable, or unwilling to express. A way of assessing which families could benefit from external support would be invaluable. Smith (1979) did look at this area, including measures such as the types of questions and statements utilised, and requests for, and giving of, information. These measures were applied to videotaped interviews carried out pre- and post-intervention. Further work is needed, however, and there are numerous methodological problems involved in this area of research. As well as assessing the need for intervention, one

148

also needs to consider the most appropriate form for that intervention to take, and, crucially, the timing of any input.

WHEN TO INTERVENE

In crisis

Several writers have discussed the stages through which a family goes in coping with a crisis, such as stroke, in one of their members. Shontz (1965), for example, described the stages as shock, realisation, retreat and finally acknowledgement. Figure 9.1 hypothesises the way in which emotions and behaviours alter through these stages in response to the sudden onset of a communication impairment in an adult family member.

Figure 9.1: Stages in reaction to crisis of onset

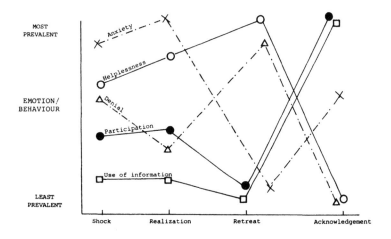

Source: Webster and Newhoff *in* Aging: Communication Processes and Disorders, D.S. Beasley & G. Albyn Davis (eds). Copyright 1981, Grune and Stratton Inc., based on Shontz, F, *Volta Review* 1965 67 364–70.

Lubinski suggests the way in which the patient's level (crisis, recuperation, rehabilitation, residual disability and, when necessary, institutionalisation) affects the family and the family's needs in terms of intervention. Her outline in adapted form can

Figure 9.2: Patient stages and effects on family

Patient stage	Effect on family	Family needs	
Severe Illness/ crisis	Fear, shock, anxiety, guilt, grieving, over concern, helplessness.	Emotional support for whole family.	
Recuperation	Adoption of new roles. Search for help. Relief after acute stage.	Education about disorder. Motivate family to work together.	
Rehabilitation	Expectation of 'cure'. New roles stabilise and may lead to isolation from friends and community. Physical changes in home. Financial concerns.	Support but emphasis on self reliance. Involvement in rehabilitation. Definition of realistic prognosis. Outline of available help. Planning for future.	Return to pre-crisis state
Residual disability	Over protection. Isolation of primary carer. Reduction in motivation. Reduction in intimacy. Resentment. Health problems.	Stress patient's independence. Stress *personal* abilities and needs. Consistent 'normal' environment. Assume regular activities. Reinforce coping strategies. Opportunity for continued emotional support.	Stabilisation
Institutionalisation	Guilt: contact raises anxiety. Discomfort with setting. Reduction in contact. Loss of companionship. Further role changes.	Help in decision making. Awareness of alternatives. Encouragement to visit and have patient home for holiday. Setting realistic goals.	Deterioration

Source: Adapted from R. Lubinski (unpublished, 1984)

be seen in Figure 9.2 and is particularly relevant to the needs of the families of older handicapped people.

Often, the family see the speech therapist early post-onset, and are offered explanations; later they deny being given explanations, or react in such a way as to suggest that the situation was not explained. This is thought to be the result of mistiming of intervention, when the family are too shocked to assimilate explanations and information, and need basic emotional support and a listening ear. It may be that information is only truly effective once the stage of acknowledgement is reached, but explanations and education about the disorder can be usefully offered as the immediate crises passes and the reality begins to hit home after the initial shock and numbness.

Some communication disorders, most notably perhaps aphasia, are of a nature difficult for lay people to understand, and many relatives are (as Schewan and Cameron found (1984)) unaware of the reasons for and the extent of the difficulties. This can lead to increased confidence (both patient and families tend to view aphasia, for example, more optimistically than the speech therapist according to Muller *et al.* (1983) and Schewan and Cameron (1984)) or to unrealistic expectations and interactions.

The timing of attempts to involve the family in rehabilitation is also important. Davis and Baggs (1984) say that the family can be used to participate in activities and to monitor practice, as well as to offer emotional support. However, if attempts are made to involve them at the stage of crisis or of realisation, it is likely that they will have difficulty in setting realistic goals for the patient. Schuell, Jenkins and Junenez-Pabon (1964), among others, has stressed the need for counselling to enable individuals to accept realistic aims, but until something is understood of the nature of the disorder, and the expectation of a 'cure' discussed, this will not be possible.

Once the situation has been accepted, albeit not welcomed, the family can be considered in the light of active helpers. However, the therapist will need to discover as much as possible about previous communication patterns and relationships, by observation, informal interview or questionnaire. There will be families in which the attempt to involve them in rehabilitation will be counterproductive. For example, a handicapped person may be unable to accept a spouse in the role of teacher.

In gradual onset

The stages of reaction to a communication disorder of gradual onset will be somewhat different from those resulting from an acute crisis. The patient with dementia, for example, will develop difficulties in communication which creep up on the partner and family insidiously. There will be frustration and irritation, which feelings are often exaggerated as the family are not warned that communication will be affected by the disease. Behaviours are mislabelled, and the whole relationship suffers as a result. Similarly, the gradual onset of a hearing loss will often lead to frustration and anger within the family.

The acceptance of gradually occurring changes may develop as the condition progresses, as Webster and Newhoff (1981) suggest, without affecting the family stability. However, if explanations and support are not available, there may never be real acceptance of the situation or, indeed, if explanations are not updated in the case of progressive disorders such as dementia.

TYPES OF INTERVENTION

Intervention may take the form of individual or group support, both of which have advantages and a role to play.

Individual intervention

The obvious advantage of working with the individual family or carer is that all the information given and received will be directly applicable. The family will have the opportunity to ask questions which may be of a personal nature, and to talk about their own response to the crisis. The therapist can discuss specific details of the patient's condition, and outline the course of therapy and any part the family might play in rehabilitation.

Assessment of the family

It will be valuable if the therapist can observe the family and the older handicapped individual together. A mental checklist (considering such factors as whether one member communicates more with the subject, whether this alters in different situations, whether conversation is restricted to concrete rather than emotive subjects, and so on) can help to structure direct observations, and indicate whether the family can be asked to participate in active rehabilitation work. Observation can also show up areas which need to be more thoroughly explained.

Not all families view communication in the same way, and it can be useful to ask questions about communication within the home. Some appear to have little verbal communication; others depend to a large extent on linguistic skills and the use of quite complex linguistic skills such as sarcasm and analogy. The answers to such questions will often influence the therapist's aims and the content of any intervention. Another area which needs to be assessed is the family's understanding of the nature of the disorder, and following this their expectations (both of the patient and of therapy), in order to correct any misconceptions and offer appropriate counselling towards realistic aims.

The therapist will need to know how the family is already coping, and whether there are physical or emotional sequelae of the caring role which might benefit from additional health or social service input.

Explanations and advice

Explanations must be carefully geared to the level of the particular family being considered, especially in relation to the language and terminology employed by the therapist. It is easy to fall into the trap of professional jargon, and to frighten the members of the family, who feel unable to ask for an explanation that they can understand. This is important for speech therapists who employ words in common usage which have a more specific professional meaning, such as 'speech' and 'language'.

A brief preliminary outline of the communication process is valuable, to illustrate exactly how the carer's behaviour can affect the patient's attempts to communicate, and that the balance can be maintained if one participant has difficulty, by the other adapting his communicative behaviours. Written information will allow the family to digest it in their own time, and sort out any questions they need to ask.

If the members of the family are to be actively involved in rehabilitation, specific advice will be needed, again geared to their level. It is important not just to provide the exercise or task that they are to undertake with the patient, but also the reasoning behind that activity, which will often not be obvious to a layman, especially if the aims are more abstract and indirectly related to communication (as in attention building, for example). Those families who it is felt best not to ask to work directly with the patient will still need advice and support on how best to encourage the handicapped person, and how to create the optimal environment for him. Some general suggestion sheets are offered in the appendix to Chapter 8 (p. 140).

Counselling

Many families find it difficult to come to terms with their changed life-style — perhaps especially because the changes are forced upon them. Some of the emotional reactions that can result have already been mentioned: the anxiety at enforced role shifts, the anger and resentment and subsequent guilt that they feel towards the handicapped person, and so on. They should be given space and time to talk about their own feelings in a non-judgemental setting. It is much more likely that problems can be resolved if their negative feelings are recognised, accepted and discussed. The influence of the family on rehabilitation efforts should not be underestimated, and nor should the family's emotional needs within that relationship.

If there are underlying conflicts which may have existed pre-morbidly, the speech therapist may well feel that counselling from a more experienced source is needed and can refer on to the appropriate agency. The question of counselling was discussed more fully in Chapter 3.

Group intervention

Working within a group can be a useful way to approach the family who is adjusting to a handicapped member. It provides the opportunity to gain support and information from others who face similar difficulties, and indeed the knowledge that there are others in a similar situation can be beneficial of itself. Schewan and Cameron (1984) found that spouses of aphasics rated this as one of the most useful results of speech therapy, the others being teaching how to work with the patient, providing psychological support and giving general information on services available.

The group is a useful forum for explaining the causes and

nature of communication disorders, and for discussion around this information. However, Newhoff and Davis ran a 'spouse intervention program' in 1978, and found that the need for basic information was less important than gaining the support and understanding of other group members.

Organisation

Groups require careful planning and preliminary enquiry as to the needs of that group and the best format to follow. Often a multidisciplinary approach will be adopted, rather than a group being organised and run by members of only one discipline or profession. This will, of course, depend on the nature of the group, and on the personal interest of individual workers. They may be 'open' to all comers, or 'closed' in that members attend by invitation. They may be information-giving (with speakers and more formal teaching) or supportive, or an amalgam of the two approaches. They may be time-limited with a set number of sessions planned, or open-ended, without a predetermined end to the course of meetings. They may meet frequently or occasionally. They may or may not include the patient as well as the carer(s).

It is important that such variations are evaluated, and that individual groups assess how well they have served their intended function, in order that changes may be made as and when appropriate. Various groups have been described in the literature. Hausman (1979) looked at short-term groups for those looking after elderly parents. The aims were to balance their responsibilities to self, to patient and to family, to make decisions related to level of involvement, and to work through past conflicts. The chosen form was for the group to be time-limited, closed, and task oriented. Unfortunately, the evaluation ('useful') was anecdotal rather than objectively assessed, and not carried out by unbiased assessors.

Greene *et al.* (1982) did attempt to look at the effects of dementia upon relatives, using a questionnaire upon which factor analysis was used to create scales which he named 'personal distress', 'degree of life upset' and 'negative feelings towards the elderly patient'. These scales were applied pre- and post-intervention in order to evaluate the effect of the group. In general, however, as Platt (1985) points out, there are few studies of the value of groups for carers that are not deficient in methodological or conceptual organisation. This is true for groups aiming at carers of elderly, of dementing, or of communicatively impaired relatives.

Evaluation of the group means pre- and post-measures are necessary. These measures may take the form of attitude questionnaires, or be indices of knowledge, which should then reveal changes in attitude, or in awareness of available support services or in general understanding of a disorder. Direct observation can be used to evaluate behaviour change in the relative's approach to the 'patient', using checklists or rating scales. However the group is evaluated, it will be important to use an outside assessor in order to avoid the bias of those who are involved in running the group.

Groups will obviously vary, both in format and content, depending on their *raison d'être*. Communication difficulty may be the reason for a group, in the case of a primary disorder such as aphasia; or may be just one of the reasons, in the case, for example, of Alzheimer's disease or other dementing conditions. Thus, the content in the latter will be much wider, and include other aspects of care and management.

In summary, one cannot overstress the impact that the family has upon the communicatively impaired older person, nor the impact of that person upon his or her family or other carer(s). As Sheldon (1982) says, 'Families are still the best asset the community has in caring for the elderly — capitalising on this makes economic as well as human sense'.

10

The State of the Art

Communication problems, at any age, can lead to emotional and psychological difficulties both for the sufferer and their families and friends. The lack of awareness in the general public, and in medical and social service workers, of how pervasive is the human need to communicate, and therefore how agonising the loss of that ability can be — combined with the invisible nature of the handicap — has resulted in many communicatively impaired people becoming isolated and feeling 'worthless'. Such outcomes are often exaggerated in the case of older people, who must also face numerous other changes in their way of life, and in the way others perceive them. The words of Sartre who reflected that 'My old age is other people' seem particularly poignant.

There is no doubt that speech and language clinicians have altered in their approach to working with older people over the last fifteen years or so. It is generally accepted that the elderly population does have special needs in terms of assessment and management of their communication disorders. Some of these needs stem from the direct influence of the aging process; others are indirectly related to aging, such as the likelihood of changed living environments and altered family patterning. However despite the recognition that older people require a different approach — often a strikingly different approach — little has been done to rationalise, determine methods, and evaluate those methods. The state of the art is that there are still more questions to ask than answers to be found. As so often happens in research, the work to date has served to throw up more and more questions and avenues of exploration. This situation makes it an exciting field in which to be involved, but also a frustrating one at times.

Perhaps the most important principle the speech therapist needs to hold is a belief in the need to evaluate his or her role, particularly those parts of that role that have been described as 'indirect'. Effective evaluation can only result from a more objective delineation of aims and methods, and there is no doubt that different evaluation procedures will be necessary for different aspects of the care of older communicatively impaired individuals. It is not enough to know intuitively that one is having an influence either on a person's communicative behaviours, or on their overall quality of life. Speech therapists must justify their work to administrators, other disciplines working with older people, and to the clients themselves.

The aged population, as has been stated, is not a homogeneous group, and the speech therapist must also be aware of the enormous racial and cultural differences, for example, that will impinge upon each client's needs for and response to therapy. The ability successfully to select the appropriate method for each client is a skill born not only of increased theoretical knowledge, but of clinical experience and intuition.

The future, born out of the necessity of the enormous increase in the numbers of older people, looks more hopeful in that there have been alterations in the philosophy of care applied to this population, and that attempts are being made to educate and inform people about the aging process. This bodes well for the quality of life of elderly people, but only if the new philosophy is translated into practical methods of care. That section of the aged population which suffers from communication impairment both need, and have a right to, speech therapists who are enthusiastic and concerned, and objective in their approach to therapy. There are many questions still to be asked, many answers to be found.

References

Adelson, R., Nasti, A., Sprafkin, J.N., Marinelli, R., Primavera, L.H. and Gorman, B.S. (1982) Behavioural ratings of health professionals' interactions with the geriatric patient. *Gerontologist, 22*, 277–81

Ainsworth, T. (1977) Effects of institutionalisation on the aged. Aspens Systems Corp, Rockville, MD

Albert, M.L. (1978) Subcortical dementia. In R. Katzman, R.D. Terry and K.L. Bick (eds), *A.D.: Senile dementia and related disorders*, Raven Press, New York

Alen-Buckley, C., Stevens, S. and Davis, A. (1982) Communicating with elderly patients. *Remedial Therapist*, June 11

Allman, P. (1982) Psychosocial aspects of aging. In M. Edwards (ed.), *Communication changes in elderly people*, College of Speech Therapists, London

Artes, R. and Hoops, R. (1976) Problems of aphasic and non-aphasic stroke patients as identified and evaluated by patient's wives. In Y. Lebrun and R. Hoops (eds), *Recovery in aphasics*, Swetz and Zeitlinger, Amsterdam

Bamford, J. (1982) Hearing and aging. In M. Edwards (ed.), *Communication changes in elderly people*. College of Speech Therapists, London

Bayles, K.A. (1984a) Analysis of written discourse in dementia patients. Paper presented at 12th Annual International Neuropsychological Society Meeting, Houston, Texas, February 1984

Bayles, K.A,. (1984b) Language and dementia. In A. Holland (ed.), *Language disorders in adults*, College Hill Press, San Diego.

Bayles, K.A. (1986) Management of neurogenic communication disorders associated with dementia. In R. Chapey (ed.), *Language intervention strategies in adult aphasia*, 2nd edn, Williams and Wilkins, Baltimore, pp. 472–73

Bayles, K.A. and Boone, D.R. (1982) The potential of language tasks for identifying senile dementia. *Journal of Speech and Hearing Disorders, 47*, 210–17

Bayles, K.A. and Tomoeda, C.K. (1983) Confrontation naming impairment in dementia. *Brain and Language, 19*, 98–114

Bayles, K.A. and Tomoeda, C.K. (1984) Analysis of written discourse in dementia patients. Paper presented at the 12th Annual International Neuropsychological Society meeting Houston, Texas, February 1984

Bayles, K.A., Tomoeda, C.K. and Caffrey, J.T. (1982) Language and dementia producing diseases. *Communication Disorders, 7*, (10), 131–46

Bayles, K.A., Tomoeda, C.K., Kaszniak, A.W., Stem, L.Z. and Eagans, K.K. (1985) Verbal perseveration of dementia patients. *Brain and Language, 25*, 102–16

Belmore, S.A. (1981) Age related changes in processing explicit and implicit language. *Journal of Gerontology, 36* (3), 316–22

Bengstson, V.L., Kasschau, P.L. and Ragan, P.K. (1977) The impact of social structure on aging individuals. In J.E. Birren and K.W. Schaie (eds), *Handbook of the psychology of aging,* Van Nostrand Reinhold, New York

Benjamin, B.J. (1982) Phonological performance in gerontological speech. *Journal of Psycholinguistic Research, 11*, (2), 159–67

Bennett, R. (1963) The meaning of institutional life. *Gerontologist, 3* (3), 117–24

Bernardini, L. (1985) Effective communication as an intervention for sensory deprivation in the elderly client. *Topics in Nursing,* Jan.

Beverly, E.V. (1975) The beginning of wisdom about aging. *Geriatrics, 30,* 117–19, 122–3

Binnie, C.A., Danilof, R.G. and Buckingham, H.W. (1982) Phonetic disintegration in a five year old following sudden hearing loss. *Journal of Speech and Hearing Disorders, 47,* 181–9

Blessed, F., Tomlinson, B.E. and Roth, M. (1968) The association between quantitative measures of dementia and of senile change in the cerebral grey matter of elderly subjects. *British Journal of Psychology, 114,* 797–881

Blood, I. and Danhauer, J.L. (1976) Are we meeting the needs of our hearing aid users? *American Speech-Hearing Association,* 343–7

Bloomer, H. (1960) Communication problems among aged county hospital patients. *Geriatrics, 15,* 291–5

Boone, D.R. (1977) *The voice and voice therapy.* Prentice Hall, Englewood Cliffs, New Jersey

Botwinick, J. (1973) *Aging and behaviour.* Springer Publishing Co., New York

Bowles, N.L. and Poon, L.W. (1985) Aging and retrieval of words in semantic memory. *Journal of Gerontology, 40,* 71–7

Brinson, W.S. (1983) Speechreading in practice. In W.J. Watts (ed.), *Rehabilitation and acquired deafness,* Croom Helm, London

Brocklehurst, J.C. and Tucker, J.S. (1980) *Progress in geriatric day care.* King Edwards Fund, London

Brumfitt, S.M. (1985) Another side to therapy. *Bulletin of the College of Speech Therapists,* May

Burke, D.M. and Light, L.L. (1981) Memory and aging: the role of retrieval processes. *Psychological Bulletin, 980,* 513–46

Butler, R. (1963) The life review: an interpretation of reminiscence in the aged. *Psychiatry, 26,* 65–76

Caird, F.I. and Williamson, J. (1986) *The eye and its disorders in the elderly.* Wright, Bristol

Caporael, L.R., Lukaszewski, M.P. and Cuthbertson, G.H. (1983) Secondary baby talk: judgements by the institutionalised elderly and their care givers. *Journal of Personality and Social Psychology, 44,* (4), 746–54

Cattell, R.B. (1943) The measurement of adult intelligence. *Psychological Bulletin, 40,* 153–93

Chaffee, C.E. (1967) Rehabilitation needs of nursing home patients:

160

REFERENCES

A report of a survey. *Rehabilitation Literature, 18,* 377–89

Chapey, R., Lubinski, R., Chapey, G. and Salzburg, A. (1979) Survey of speech, language and hearing services in nursing home settings. *Long Term Care and Health Services Administration Quarterly,* Winter, 307–16

Chermak, G. and Jinks, M. (1981) Counselling the hearing impaired older adult. *Drug Intelligence and Clinical Pharmacy, 15,* May

Chown (1977) Morale careers and personal potentials. In J.E. Birren and K.W. Schaie (eds), *Handbook of the psychology of aging,* Van Nostrand Reinhold, New York

Clifford Rose, F. and Capildeo, R. (1981) *Stroke — the facts!* Oxford University Press, Oxford and New York

Cohen, G. (1979) Language comprehension in old age. *Cognitive Psychology, 11,* 412–29

Cohen, G. and Faulkner, D. (1983) Word recognition: age differences in contextual facilitation effects. *British Journal of Psychology, 74,* 239–51

Cole, M., Wright, D. and Banker, B.Q. (1979) Familial aphasia due to Pick's disease. *Annals of Neurology, 6,* 158

Cooper, L.D. and Rigrodsky, S. (1979) Verbal training to improve explanations of conservation with aphasic adults. *Journal of Speech and Hearing Research, 22,* 818–28

Corso, J. (1971) Sensory processes and age effects in normal adults. *Journal of Gerontology, 26,* 90–105

Corso, J.F., (1977) Auditory perception and communication. In J.E. Birren and K.W. Schaie (eds), *Handbook of the psychology of aging,* Van Nostrand Reinhold, New York

Cox, D.E. and Swan, S. (1978) Speech therapy for geriatric patients. *Bulletin of the College of Speech Therapists,* April

Crapper, D.R., Krishnan, S.S. and Quittkat, S. (1976) Aluminium neurofibrillary degeneration and Alzheimer's disease. *Brain, 99,* 67–80

Crombie, A.L. (1986) Cataract. In F.I. Caird and J. Williamson (eds), *The eye and its disorders in the elderly.* Wright, Bristol

Darley, F.L. (1969) Aphasia input and output disturbances in speech and language processing. Paper presented at American Speech and Hearing Association, Chicago

Davis, A.C. (1983) Hearing disorders in the population. In M.E. Lutman and M.P. Haggard (eds), *Hearing science and hearing disorders,* Academic Press, London

Davis, G.A. and Baggs, T.W. (1984) Rehabilitation of speech and language disorder. In *Gerontology and communication disorders,* ASHA Conference on Aging

Davis, G.A. and Holland, A.L. (1981) Age in understanding and treating aphasia. In D.S. Beasley and G.A. Davis (eds), *Aging: communication processes and disorders,* Grune and Stratton, New York, pp. 106–32

Davis, G.A. and Wilcox, J.M. (1981) Incorporating parameters of natural conversation in aphasia treatment. In R. Chapey (ed.),

161

REFERENCES

Language intervention strategies in adult aphasia, Williams and Wilkins, Baltimore, pp. 169–94

de Ajuriaguerra, J. and Tissot, R. (1975) Some aspects of language in various forms of senile dementia. In E.H. Lenneberg and E. Lenneberg (eds), *Foundations of Language Development, 1*, Academic Press Inc. (London) Ltd

Denney, N.W. (1981) Adult cognitive development. In D.S. Beasley and G.A. Davis (eds), *Aging: communication processes and disorders*, Grune and Stratton, New York, pp. 123–38

Dolen, L.S. and Beavison, D.J. (1982) Social interaction and social cognition in aging: a contextual analysis. *Human Development, 25*, 430–42

Eaton-Griffiths, V. (1975) Volunteer scheme for dysphasia and allied problems in stroke patients. *British Medical Journal, 13*, 633–5

Egan, G. (1981) *The skilled helper*, Brooks/Cole, Monterey, California

Eisdorfer, C. and Stotsky, B.A. (1977) Intervention, treatment and rehabilitation of psychological disorders. In D.S. Birren and K.W. Schaie (eds), *Handbook of the psychology of aging*, Van Nostrand Reinhold, New York

Eisenson, J. (1954) *Examining for aphasia*. The Psychological Corp., New York

Emerick, L. (1971) *Appraisal of language disturbance*. Northern Michigan University Press, Marquette, Michigan

Emerick, L.L. and Hatten, J.T. (1974) *Diagnosis and evaluation in speech pathology*, Prentice Hall, Englewood Cliffs, New Jersey

Enderby, P.M. (1983) *Frenchay dysarthria assessment*, College Hill Press, San Diego

Engen, T. (1977) Taste and smell. In J.E. Birren and K.W. Schaie (eds), *Handbook of the psychology of aging*, Van Nostrand Reinhold, New York

Erikson, E.H. (1968) *Identity: youth and crisis*. W.W. Norton, New York

Ewartson, H.W. (1974) Hearing rehabilitation in Denmark. *Hearing instruments, 25* (9), 20–1

Fallot, R.D. (1979–80) The impact of mode of verbal reminiscing in later adulthood. *International Journal of Aging and Human Development, 10* (4) pp. 285–400

Fozard, J.L., Wolf, E., Bell, B., McFarland, R.A. and Podolsky, S. (1977) In J.E. Birren and K.W. Schaie (eds), *Handbook of the psychology of aging*, Van Nostrand Reinhold, New York

Fox, E.M. (1985) Community resources and the demented patient. *Geriatric Medicine,* April

Franks, A.S.T. (1982) Oro-facial changes connected with normal aging. In M. Edwards (ed.), *Communication changes in elderly people*, College of Speech Therapists Monograph, London

Freer, C. (1985) Old myths. *Lancet, i*

Freestone, G.M. (1983) The basis of practical auditory training. In W.J. Watts (ed.), *Rehabilitation and acquired deafness*, Croom Helm, London

Gabell, A. (1981) Death wish. *Nursing Mirror*, Oct. 21

Gacek, R. (1975) Degenerative hearing loss in aging. In W. Fields (ed.), *Neurological and sensory disorders in the elderly*, Stratton International Medical Book Corp., New York

Gardner, H., Zunif, E.B., Berry, T. and Baker, E. (1976) Visual communication in aphasia. *Neuropsychologia, 14*, 275–92

Garstecki, D.C. (1981) Aural rehabilitation for the aging adult. In D.S. Beasley and G.A. Davis (eds), *Aging: communication processes and disorders*, Grune and Stratton, New York

Gewirth, L.R. Schindler, A.G. and Hier, D.B. (1984) Altered patterns of word associations in dementia and aphasia. *Brain and Language, 21*, 307–17

Gifford, W. (1980) Talking about dying. *Community Outlook/Nursing Times*, Nov. 13

Goffman, E. (1960) Characteristics of total institutions. In M.R. Stein, A.J. Vidich and D.M. White (eds), *Identity and anxiety survival of the person in mass society*, The Free Press, Glencoe, Illinois

Goldfarb, A.I. (1975) Memory and aging. In R. Goldman and M. Rockstein (eds), *The physiology and pathology of human aging*, Academic Press, New York

Goodglass, H. and Kaplan, E. (1983) *The assessment of aphasia and related disorders*. Lea and Febiger, Philadelphia

Gordon, D.M. (1965) Eye problems of the aged. *Journal of American Geriatric Society, 13*, 398–417

Gray, A. (1982) The challenge of multidisciplinary teamwork. *College of Speech Therapists Bulletin, 358*

Greene, G., Smith, C., Gardiner, M. and Timbury, C. (1982) Measuring behavioural disturbance of elderly demented patients in the community and its effects on relatives: a factor analytical study. *Age and Aging, 11*, 121–6

Greene, M.C.L. (1982) Aging of the voice — a review. In M. Edwards (ed), *Communication changes in elderly people*, College of Speech Therapists, Monograph, London

Haspiel, M., Clement, J.R. and Haspiel, G.S. (1972) Aural rehabilitation for hard of hearing adults. *S.F.V.A.* (unpublished).

Hausman, C.P. (1979) Short-term counselling groups for people with elderly parents. *Gerontologist, 19*, 102–7

Helm, N. and Barresi, B. (1980) Voluntary control of involuntary utterances: a treatment approach for severe aphasia. In R.H. Brookshire (ed.), *Clinical aphasiology Conference Proceedings*, BRK Publications, Minneapolis

Helm-Estabrooks, N. and Albert, M. (1980) Visual action therapy for global aphasia. Veterans Administration Merit Review Grant

Helm-Estabrooks, N., Fitzpatrick, P. and Barresi, B. (1982) Response of an agrammatic patient to a syntax stimulation program for aphasia. *Journal of Speech and Hearing Disorders, 46*, 422–7

Herr, J.L. and Weakland, J.H. (1979) *Counselling elders and their families*. Springer Publishing Co., New York

High, W., Fairbanks, G. and Glorig, A. (1964) A scale for self assessment of hearing. *Journal of Speech and Hearing Disorders, 29*, 215–30

REFERENCES

Holland, A. (1980) *Communicative abilities in daily living*, University Park Press, Baltimore

Hughston, G.A. and Merriam, S.M. (1982) Reminiscence: a non-formal technique for improving cognitive functioning in the aged. *International Journal of Aging and Human Development, 15* (2), 139–49

Isaacs, B. (1977) Five years experience of a stroke unit. *Health Bulletin (Edinburgh), 35*, 95–8

Kane, R.L., Kane, R.A. and Arnold, S. (1985) Prevention and the elderly: risk factors. *Health Services Research, 19*, 945–1006

Keenan, J.S. (1979) Communication disorders and institutionalised geriatric patients. *Communication Disorders An Audio Journal for Continuing Education, 4*

Keenan, J.S. and Brassell, E.G. (1975) *Aphasia language performance scales*. Pinnacle Press, Murfeesborough, Tennessee

Kellaher, L.A., Peace, S.M. and Willcocks, D.M. (1985) Living in homes: a consumer view of old people's homes. *Centre for Environmental and Social Services in Aging/BASE*, Keele, Staffs

Kenshalo, D.R. (1977) Age changes in touch, vibration, temperature, kinesthesis and pain sensitivity. In J.E. Birren and K.W. Schaie (eds), *Handbook of the psychology of aging*, Van Nostrand Reinhold, New York

Kertesz, A. (1979) *Western aphasia battery*. Grune and Stratton, New York

Kinsella, G. and Duffy, F. (1978) The spouse of the aphasic patient. In D. Lebrun and R. Hoops (eds), *The Management of Aphasia*, Swets and Zeitlinger, Amsterdam, pp. 26–49

Kirschner, H.S., Webb, W.G. and Kelly, K.P. (1982) The naming disorder of dementia. *American Academy of Neurology paper.*

Kleemeier, R.W. (1959) Behaviour and the organisation of the bodily and the external environment. In J.G. Birren (ed), *Handbook of aging and the individual*, University of Chicago Press, Chicago

Klotz, P. (1963) La surdite du troisieme age. *Readoption, 102*, 27–31

Knox, A.B. (1981) Adult development. In D.S. Beasley and G.A. Davis (eds), *Aging: communication processes and disorders*, Grune and Stratton, New York

Kubler-Ross, E. (1974) *On death and dying*, Macmillan, New York

Langyut, C.L., Madison, C.L. and Weir, I.L. (1983) A survey study of resistance to discharge from speech-language therapy. *Journal of Communication Disorders, 16*, 189–200

Leutenegger,R.R. (1975) *Patient care and rehabilitation of communicatively impaired adults*, Charles C. Thomas, Springfield, Illinois

Linebaugh, C.W. (1983) Treatment of anomic aphasia. In W.H. Perkins (ed.), *Current therapy of communication disorders: Language handicaps in adults*. Thieme-Stratton, New York

Logemann, J. (1983) *Evaluation and treatment of swallowing disorders*, College Hill Press, San Diego

Logue, R.D. and Dixon, M.M. (1979) Word association and the anomic response: analysis and treatment. In R.H. Brookshire (ed.),

REFERENCES

Clinical aphasiology: Conference Proceedings, BRK Publications, Minneapolis

Lubinski, R. (1978–79) Why so little interest in whether or not old people talk? *International Journal of Aging and Human Development, 9* (3), 237–44

Lubinski, R. (1981a) Language and aging: an environmental approach to intervention. *Aspens Systems Corp./Topics in Language Disorders,* Sept., 89–97

Lubinski, R. (1981b) Speech, language and audiology programs in home health care agencies and nursing homes. In D.S. Beasley and G.A. Davis (eds), *Aging: communication processes and disorders,* Grune and Stratton, New York, pp. 339–56

Lubinski, R. (1984) Environmental considerations for the institutionalised demented patient. Paper at NYSSHA Convention

Lubinski, R., Morrison, E.B. and Rigrodsky, S. (1981) Perception of spoken communication by elderly chronically ill patients in an institutional setting. *Journal of Speech and Hearing Disorders, 46,* 405–12

Luria, A.R. (1970) *Traumatic aphasia,* Vitgeverij Mouton, The Hague, Netherlands

Madden, D.J. and Nebes, R.D. (1980) Aging and the development of automaticity in visual search. *Developmental Psychology, 16,* 377–84

Malone, L. (1969) Expressed attitudes of families of aphasics. *Journal of Speech and Hearing Disorders, 34,* 146–50

Marmar, M.F., Crombie, A.L. and Wilson, W. (1986) Visual changes with age. In F.I. Caird and J. Williamson (eds), *The eye and its disorders in the elderly,* Wright, Bristol

Marston, N. and Gupta, H. (1977) Interesting the old. *Community Care,* 16 Nov., 26–8

Martin, J.C. (1983) Health care for the elderly: what does the future hold? *Dimensions,* Nov., 4–5

McMahon, A.W. and Rhudick, P.J. (1964) Reminiscing: adaptational significance in the aged. *Archives of General Psychiatry, 10,* 292–8

Mergler, N.L. and Faust, M. (1984–85) Storytelling as an age dependent
skill. *International Journal of Aging and Human Development, 20* (3), 205–8

Mesulam, M.M. (1982) Slowly progressive aphasia without generalised dementia. *Annals of Neurology, 11,* 592–8

Meyerson, M.D. (1976) The effects of aging on communication. *Journal of Gerontology, 31* (1)

Moon, R.E. (1984) The home help service and speech therapy. Unpublished survey

Morris, J.N., Sherwood, S. and Mor, V. (1984) An assessment tool for use in identifying functionally vulnerable persons in the community. *Gerontologist, 24* (4), 373–9

Motor Neurone Disease Association (1984) *Counselling the M.N.D. patient and family.* Motor Neurone Disease Association, UK

Mueller, P.B. and Peters, T.J. (1981) Needs and services in geriatric speech-language pathology and audiology. *Proceedings of the American Speech and Hearing Association*, Sept., 627–32

Mulhall, D.J. (1978) Dysphasic stroke patients and the influence of their relatives. *British Journal of Disorders of Communication, 13*, 127–34

Muller, D.J., Code, C. and Mingford, J. (1983) Predicting psychosocial adjustment to aphasia. *British Journal of Disorders of Communication, 18* (1)

Murphy, E. (1985) The GP and the psychogeriatrician. *Geriatric Medicine*, May

Mysak, E.D. and Hanley, T.D. (1958) Aging processes in speech, pitch and duration characteristics. *Journal of Gerontology, 13*, 309–13

Nerbonne, M., Schow, R., Goset, F. and Bliss, A. (1976) Prevalence of conductive pathology in a nursing home population (unpublished study)

Neugarten, B. and Gutman, D.L. (1958) Age and sex roles in personality in middle age. *Psychology Monograph, 72* (71), no. 470

Newhoff, M.N. and Davis, G.A. (1978) A spouse intervention program. In R.H. Brookshire (ed), *Clinical aphasiology: Conference Proceedings*, BRK Publications, Minnesota

Norris, M.L. and Cunningham, D.R. (1981) Social impact of hearing loss in the aged. *Journal of Gerontology, 36* (6), 727–9

Norris, E.I. and Eileh, A. (1982) Reminiscence groups, *Nursing Times*, Aug 11

Nuru, N., (1985) Institutionalised people: can we do a better job? *ASHA*, Jan 35–7

Obler, L.K. and Albert, M.L. (1981a) Language in the elderly aphasic and in the dementing patient. In M. Taylor Sarno (ed), *Acquired aphasia*, Academic Press, New York

Obler, L.K. and Albert, M.L. (1981b) Language and aging: a neurobehavioural analysis. In D.S. Beasley and G.A. Davis (eds), *Aging: communication processes and disorders*, Grune and Stratton, New York

Obler, L.K., Woodward, S. and Albert, M.L. (1984) Changes in cerebral lateralisation in aging. *Neuropsychologia, 22* (2), 235–40

Obler, L.K., Albert, M.L., Nicholas, M. and Helm-Esterbrooks, N. (1985) Empty speech in Alzheimers disease and fluent aphasia. *Journal of Speech and Hearing Research, 28*, 405–10

Obler, L.K., Woodward, S. and Albert, M.L. (1984) Changes in cerebral lateralisation in aging. *Neuropsychologia, 22* (2), 235–40

O'Connell, P. and O'Connell, E. (1978) Speech and language pathology services in a skilled nursing facility. *Proceedings of the American Speech and Hearing Association*, Nov.

Oradei, D.M. and Waite, J.S. (1974) Group psychotherapy with stroke patients during the immediate recovery phase. *American Journal of Orthopsychiatry, 44*, 386–95

Orzeck, A.Z. (1964) *Orzeck aphasia evaluation*. Western Psychological Services, Los Angeles

REFERENCES

Ouslander, J.G. and Beck, J.C. (1982) Defining the health problems of the elderly. *Annual Review Public Health, 3*, 55–83

Oxtoby, M. (1982) *Parkinsons's disease patients and their social needs*, Parkinsons Disease Society, London

Page,E.R. (1967) Speech and language characteristics of institutionalised and geriatric patients. In *Proceedings of 7th International Congress of Gerontology, 4*, Viennese Medical Academy, Vienna

Parker, A. (1983) Speech conservation. In W.J. Watts (ed), *Rehabilitation and acquired deafness*, Croom Helm, London

Perkin, G.D. (1986) *Basic neurology*. Ellis Horwood, Chichester

Perrotta, P. and Meacham, J.A. (1981–82) Can a reminiscing intervention alter depression and self esteem? *International Journal of Aging and Human Development, 14* (1), 23–40

Pitt, B. (1982) *Psychogeriatrics*, 2nd edn, Churchill Livingstone, Edinburgh and New York

Pirozzolo, F.J., Hansch, E.C., Mortimer, J.A., Webster, D.D. and Kuskowski, M.A. (1982) Dementia in Parkinson's disease; a neuropsychological analysis. *Brain and Cognition, 1*, 78–83

Platt, S. (1985) Measuring the burden of psychiatric illness on the family: an evaluation of some rating scales. *Psychological Medicine, 15*, 383–93

Pollock, M. and Hornabrook, R.W. (1966) The prevalence, natural history and dementia of Parkinson's disease. *Brain, 89*, 429–48

Porch, B.E. (1973) *Porch index of communicative ability*. Consulting Psychologists Press, Palo Alto, California

Posner, J. and Ventry, I. (1977) Relationship between comfortable loudness levels for speech and speech discrimination in sensorineural hearing loss. *Journal of Speech and Hearing Disorders, 42*, 370–5

Powell Lawton, M. (1977) The impact of environment of aging and behaviour. In J.E. Birren and K.W. Schaie (eds), *Handbook of the psychology of aging*, Van Nostrand Reinhold, New York

Powell-Proctor, L. (1980) Reality orientation: a treatment of choice? *General Medicine*, Nov.

Ramig, L.A., (1983) Effects of physiological aging on speaking and reading rates. *Journal of Communicative Disorders, 16*, 217–26

Rennie, I.G. and Davidson, S.I. (1986) Examination of the eye in the elderly. In F.I. Caird and J. Williamson (eds), *The eye and its disorders in the elderly*, Wright, Bristol

Rimmer, L. (1982) *Reality orientation: principles and practice*, Winslow Press, Aylesbury, Bucks

Robertson, S.J. (1982) *Dysarthria profile* (privately published)

Robertson, S.J. and Thomson, F. (1984) Speech therapy in Parkinson's disease: a study of the efficacy and long term effects of intensive speech therapy. *British Journal of Disorders of Communication, 19*, 213–24

Rochford, G. (1971) A study of naming errors in dysphasia and in demented patients. *Neuropsychologia, 9*, 436–43

Rogers, C.R. (1961) *On becoming a person*, Houghton Mifflin, Boston

167

REFERENCES

Roos, N.P., Shapiro, E. and Roos, L.L. (1984) Aging and the demand for health services. *Gerontologist, 24* (1), 31–6

Rosenbek, J.C. and LaPointe, L.L. (1981) Motor speech disorders and the aging process. In D.S. Beasley and G.A. Davis (eds), *Aging: communication processes and disorders*, Grune and Stratton, New York

Rowe, J.W. (1985) Health care of the elderly. *New England Journal of Medicine, 312* (13)

Rupp, R.R., Higgins, J. and Maurer, J.F. (1977) A feasibility scale for predicting hearing aid use with older individuals. *Journal of Academic Rehabilitation and Audiology, 10*, 81–104

Russell, J. (1981) The response of a normal elderly population to the PICA test, paper presented at Special Interest Group in Geriatrics, Durham

Ryan, W.J. and Burk, K.W. (1974) Perception and acoustic correlates of aging. *Journal of Communicative Disorders, 7*

Sarno, M.T. (1969) *Functional communication profile.* Institute of Rehabilitation Medicine, New York University Medical Centre, New York

Schaie, K.W. (1977–8) Toward a stage theory of adult cognitive development. *Journal of Aging and Human Development, 8* 129–38

Schaie, K.W. and Schaie, J.P. (1977) Clinical assessment and aging. In J.E. Birren and K.W. Schaie (eds), *Handbook of the psychology of aging*, Van Nostrand Reinhold, New York

Schaier, A.H. and Cicirelli, V.G. (1976) Age differences in humour comprehension and appreciation in old age. *Journal of Gerontology, 31*, 577–82

Schewan, C.M. and Cameron, H. (1984) Communication and related problems as perceived by aphasic individuals and their spouses. *Journal of Communicative Disorders, 17*, 175–87

Schow, R.L., Christensen, J.M., Hutchinson, J.M. and Nerbonne, M.A. (1978) *Communication disorders of the aged*, University Park Press, Baltimore

Schuell, H. (1965) *The Minnesota test for differential diagnosis of aphasia.* University of Minnesota Press, Minneapolis

Schuell, H., Jenkins, J.J. and Junenez-Pabon, E. (1964) *Aphasia in adults,* Harper and Row, New York

Schuknecht, H. and Igarashi, K. (1964) Pathology of slowly progressive sensori-neural deafness. *Transactions of the American Academy of Ophthalmology and Otolaryngology, 68*, 222–42

Schwartz, M.E., Marin, O.S. and Saffran, E.M. (1979) Dissociations of language function in dementia: a case study. *Brain and Language, 7*, 277–306

Scott, S., Caird, F.I. and Williams, B.O. (1985) *Communication in Parkinson's disease*, Croom-Helm, London/Aspen Publishers, Rockville, Maryland

Shadden, B.B., Raiford, C.A. and Shadden, H.S. (1983) *Coping with communication disorders in aging*, CC Publications Inc., Tigard, Oregon, USA

Shanas, E., Townsend, P., Wedderburn, D., Fris, H., Mulhoj, P. and Stehouwer, J. (eds) (1968) *Old people in three industrial societies.* Atherton Press, New York

Shontz, F. (1965) Reactions to crisis. *Volta Review, 67,* 364–70

Shekum, L.O. and LaPointe, L.L. (1984) Production of discourse in individuals with Alzheimer's disease. *Neuropsychological Society paper at Houston,* February 1984

Sheldon, F. (1982) Supporting the supporters: working with the relatives of patients with dementia. *Age and Aging, 11,* 184–8

Skinner, C., Wirz, S., Thompson, I. and Davidson, J. (1984) *Edinburgh functional communication profile.* Winslow Press, Aylesbury, Bucks., UK

Sklar, M. (1966) *Sklar aphasia scale.* Western Psychological Services, Los Angeles

Smith, C.L. (1979) Families of communicatively impaired adults, Masters Thesis, Memphis State University

Smith, C.R. and Fay, T.H. (1977) A program of auditory rehabilitation for aged persons in a chronic disease hospital. *Proceedings of the American Speech and Hearing Association, 19,* 417–20

Smith, D.A. and Fullerton, A.M. (1981) Age differences in episodic and semantic memory in aging. In D.S. Beasley and G.A. Davis (eds), *Aging: communication processes and disorders,* Grune and Stratton, New York, pp. 139–55

Sommer, R. and Ross, H. (1958) Social interaction in a geriatric ward. *International Journal of Social Psychiatry, 4,* 128–33

Sparks, R., Helm, N. and Albert, M. (1974) Aphasia rehabilitation resulting from melodic intonation therapy. *Cortex, 10,* 303–16

Spreen, O. and Benton, A.L. (1969) *Neurosensory centre comprehensive examination for aphasia.* University of Victoria Neuropsychology Laboratory, Victoria, BC

Stevens, S. (1985a) The language of dementia in the elderly. *British Journal of Communicative Disorders, 20,* 181–90

Stevens, S. (1985b) A domiciliary service for the elderly. *College of Speech Therapists Bulletin,* Sept., no. 41

Strang, J.R., Caine, N. and Acheson, R.M. (1983) Team care of elderly patients in general practice. *British Medical Journal, 286,* 851–4

Tomlinson, B.E. (1977) Morphological changes and dementia in old age. In W.L. Smith and M. Kinsbourne (eds), *Aging and dementia,* Spectrum Publications, New York, pp. 25–56

Tompkins, C.A., Marshall, R.C. and Phillips, D.S. (1980) Aphasic patients in a rehabilitation programme: scheduling speech and language services. *Archives of Physical Medicine and Rehabilitation, 61,* June

Ventry, I.M. and Weinstein, B.E. (1982) The hearing handicap inventory for the elderly: a new tool. *Ear and Hearing, 3* (3), 128–34

Vernon, M., Griffin, D.H. and Yoken, C. (1981) Hearing loss. *Journal of Family Practice, 12* (6), 1152–8

Wallace, G.L. and Canter, G.J. (1985) Effects of personally relevant language materials on the performance of severely aphasic individuals. *Journal of Speech and Hearing Disorders, 50*, 385–90

Walker, S.A. (1984) The communicative status of older people: differentiation and rehabilitation, *International Rehabilitation and Medicine, 6*, 139–43

Walker, S.A. and Williams, B. (1980) The response of a disabled elderly population to speech therapy. *British Journal of Disorders of Communication, 15*, 1–19

Walker, S.A. (1982) Communication as a changing function of age. In M. Edwards (ed.), *Communication changes in elderly people*, College of Speech Therapists, Monograph, London

Watts, W.J. (1983) *Rehabilitation and acquired deafness*, Croom Helm, London

Webster, J. and Webster, I.W. (1977) Rehabilitation in the community. *Medical Journal of Australia, 2*, 51–6

Webster, E.J. and Newhoff, M. (1981) Intervention with families of communicatively impaired adults. In D.S. Beasley and G.A. Davis (eds), *Aging: communication processes and disorders*, Grune and Stratton, New York, pp. 229–40

Wechsler, A.F. (1977) Presenile dementia presenting as aphasia. *Journal of Neurology, Neurosurgery and Psychiatry, 40*, 303–5

Weigl, E. (1968) On the problem of cortical syndromes: experimental studies. In M.L. Simmel (ed), *The reach of the mind*. Springer, New York

Weinstock, C. and Bennett, R. (1968) Problems in communication to nurses among residents of a socially heterogenous nursing home. *Gerontologist, 8*, 72–5

Weiss, A.E. (1971) Communication needs of the geriatric population. *Journal of American Geriatric Society, 19*, 640–5

Wepman, J.M. (1976) Aphasia: language without thought or thought without language? *Proceedings of the American Speech and Hearing Association, 18*, 131–6

Wepman, J.M. and Jones, L.V. (1961) The language modalities test for aphasia. Chicago Education-Industry Service

Wertz, R.T. (1984) State of the clinical art. In A. Holland (ed.), *Language disorders in adults*, College Hill Press, San Diego

Wertz, R.T. LaPointe, L.L. and Rosenbek, J.C. (1984) *Apraxia of speech in adults*, Grune and Stratton, New York

Whitaker, H.A. (1976) A case of isolation of the language functions. In H. Whitaker and H.A. Whitaker (eds), *Studies in neurolinguistics, 2*, Academic Press, New York, pp. 1–58

Whurr, R. (1974) An aphasia screening test. Private publication

Williams, I. (1985) Social decline and vulnerability in old age. *Geriatric Medicine*, April

Williams,S.A., Denney, N.W. and Schadler, M. (1983) Elderly adults' perception of their own cognitive development during the adult years. *International Journal of Aging and Human Development, 16* (2)

Williamson, J. and Caird, F.I. (1986) Epidemiology of ocular disorders in old age. In F.I. Caird and J. Williamson (eds), *The eye and its disorders in the elderly*. Wright, Bristol

Wilson, W. (1986) Social aspects of blindness in old age. In F.I. Caird and J. Williamson (eds), *The eye and its disorders in the elderly*, Wright, Bristol

Woods, R. and Britton, P. (1985) Treatment approaches for organic disorders. In *Clinical psychology and the elderly*, Croom Helm, London/Aspen, Rockville, Maryland

Zucker, K. and Williams, P. (1977) Audiological services in an extended care facility, *Proceedings of the American Speech and Hearing Association*, Chicago

Index

acoustics 120
adaptation 90
adjustment *see* psychological adjustment
ageism *see* attitude
aging
  and attention 8–9
  and cardiovascular system 5
  and cognition 7–9
  and communication 1–24, 140
  and dementia 63–4
  and intelligence 9
  and learning ability 9
  and memory 3, 7–9
  and problem solving 9
  and respiratory system 5
  and smell 94
  and taste 94
  chronological 2
  physiological 2–5
  psychological adjustment to 47–51
  psychomotor 6–7
  psychosocial 10–11
  sensoriperceptual 5–6, 74–94, 107
  sociocultural differences 10, 157
  study of 4–5
  see also elderly people
alternative communication methods 25, 58
Alzheimer's Disease 15, 52–6 *passim*
amplification 83–5, 120
Amyotrophic Lateral Sclerosis 49–50
anarthria *see* dysarthria
aphasia
  advice to carers 143
  and cerebrovascular accident 15, 16, 20
  and dementia 19, 63–7
  and dyspraxia 25
  and elderly people 15–16, 22
  and families 146, 148, 151
  efficacy of therapy 24, 135
  functional communication in 22
  group therapy 29–30, 46
  influences on therapy 24
  intervention planning 33–34
  slowly progressive 67
  therapy techniques 23–4
aphonia *see* dysphonia
apraxia of speech *see* dyspraxia of speech
arthritis 7
articulation 13–4
assessment
  and anxiety 8, 31, 79, 91
  and attention 8
  and caution 5, 8, 31, 79, 91
  and cultural differences 8, 32
  case histories 19, 26–7, 63, 66, 90
  difficulties 31–2, 72
  in institutions 114–15
  in the community 102, 104
  materials 8, 31
  norms for elderly 3, 12, 16, 18–19, 30–2
  observation 100, 102
  performance of elderly 5, 8, 31–2, 37
  reaction time 6, 7, 9
  response rigidity 6
  see also aphasia, dementia, dysarthria, dysphonia, dyspraxia, hearing, vision
attention
  and aging 8–9
  and communication 11–12
  and dementia 57, 60, 61
  and therapy 38
attitudes
  ageism 100, 125, 129–30, 145–6
  of health and social services

132, 136
in residential homes 111,
118–19, 125
stereotypes 1, 6, 31–5 *passim*
to communication 130
audiology *see* hearing
audiometry 76–9
auditory training *see* hearing
loss

bereavement 48–50, 108
Boston Diagnostic Aphasia
Evaluation 22, 69
brain
anatomical structure 20–1,
54–5
hemispheric lateralisation 15

cancer 27–8, 49
cardiovascular system 5
cerebrovascular accident
and aphasia 15, 16, 20
and dementia 54, 66
and drug dosage 35
and dysarthria 25
and dysphagia 28
and dyspraxia 15
and family reactions 149
and Reversible Ischaemic
Neurological Deficit 17
and Transient Ischaemic
Attack 17, 54
definition 16–17
in institutions 117
incidence 17
chiropody 99
chronological aging 2
cognition
and aging 7–9, 124
and language 11–15 *passim*
52, 68–9
Schaeie model of 7
colour vision 90
communication
and aging 3–5, 11–15, 139
and emotional expression 45
and health 24–5
and learning 24–5
and memory 11–12
and sensory abilities 3–6, 15,

24–5, 82–7, 93–4
expectations 24
in institutions 110–15
normal chain 3–4, 74, 139
opportunity for 3–4, 15
see also non-verbal
communication:
assessment
communication disorders *see*
aphasia, dyarthria,
dyspraxia, dysphonia,
dementia, hearing, vision,
psychological adjustment
communicative activities of
daily living 14, 22
communicative environment
as therapy variable 39, 79,
100–5
assessment of 126–8
communication impaired 110
effect on communication 14,
24, 31, 39, 100–1
physical 107, 110, 115,
119–20
positive environment 119,
125, 154
social 39, 107
types 95–9
community services 95–9,
103–4, 106, 133–5
comprehension *see* language
confidentiality 42, 51
contrast sensitivity 89–90
coping behaviours 42, 46, 48, 60
counselling
confidentiality 42, 51
counsellor role 42–4
Egan model 40
in the community 102–3
referring on 51
relocation 108
unconditional positive regard
35, 43, 51
with communication
impaired 26, 41–2, 44–6
with elderly 47–9
with families 149–56
with hearing impaired 83–4
cultural factors 8–10, 32–4, 42,
46, 111, 145

INDEX

day care 95
death and dying 49–50
dementia
  Alzheimer's Disease 15, 52–6
    passim
  and communication 52,
    57–69 *passim,* 141
  and families 133, 152, 155–6
  and memory 52, 57, 70
  and Parkinson's Disease 56
  and perception 59, 61, 65, 70
  and Speech Therapy 65–71
    passim
  assessment 68–9
  differential diagnosis 19, 57,
    63–7
  group work 124–5
  Huntington's Chorea 56
  in institutional care 117
  incidence 54
  Jakob Creutsfeldt 56
  Korsakoff's disease 53–4
  Kuru 56
  management 30, 65–71
    passim, 133, 141
  multi-infarct 15, 54, 58, 66
  Pick's disease 53–4
  research into 71–2
  subcortical forms 54–6, 58
  symptoms 57
depression
  and communication disorder
    42
  and reminiscence 124
  in dementia 52, 57
  in elderly 10, 15
  in families 146
discharge from therapy 36–7,
    45, 100
discourse 11–13, 14
drugs
  and communication 33–4
  and health costs 2
  and hearing loss 76
  and therapy 133
  and visual impairment 35,
    91–3
  dosage problems in elderly
    34–5, 93
  in dementia 56, 68, 72

dysarthria
  and drugs 33–4
  and group therapy 30
  advice 143
  assessment 26
  counselling 42
  in cerebrovascular accident
    15–16, 20
  in dementia 58
  in hearing loss 83
  in Parkinson's Disease 17–18
dysphagia 22, 28–9
dysphasia *see* aphasia
dysphonia 15, 20, 27–8
dyspraxia of speech 15, 17, 20,
    24–5, 63

the ear 5–6, 75
echoic memory 7–8
efficacy of therapy *see*
  evaluation of therapy
elderly people
  dependency 95
  drug use 2, 33–5
  health care 2, 96, 117
  isolation 15, 29, 39, 101
  multiple pathologies 3, 26–7,
    31, 97
  psychological adjustment to
    age 47–51
  resistance to discharge 36–7
  statistics 1–2
environment *see* communicative
  environment
environmental modification
  and dementia 71
  and hearing impaired 85–6
  as a therapy variable 32
  acoustics 120
  in institutions 115, 119–20
  lighting 120
episodic memory 7–8
evaluation of therapy 39, 72,
    125, 155–8
the eye 5–6, 88–9

families
  adjustment to
    communication disordered
    45–6, 146–53

174

and dementia 67–8, 70–1
and hearing impaired 87
assessment of 67–8, 152–3
attitudes to older members
  129
communication patterns
  151–2
counselling 108, 153–4
effect on communication
  disordered 19, 147–8, 151,
  153
group work 154–6
in multidisciplinary team
  28–9, 134–6
need for support 71, 133,
  145–9, 154
roles within 146–7
sociocultural differences 145
speech therapy intervention
  28–9, 39, 70–1
timing of intervention 150–1
types of intervention 152–6
family doctor 99, 196, 133
family therapy 47
fatigueability 25–7, 31, 33, 39,
  103
functional communication 14–
  15, 22–3, 52

general practitioner *see* doctor
gesture *see* non-verbal
  communication
glare 90, 120
grammar
  and aging 11–13
  and dementia 59–60
group therapy
  evaluation of 128
  in counselling 46–7
  organisation of 29–30, 155–6
  reality orientation 71, 121,
    124–5
  reminiscence therapy 121,
    123–4
  with communication
    disordered 29–30
  with confused 123–5
  with families 154–6
  with institutions 121–5

haptic memory 7–8
hearing
  assessment 76–9
  audiology 76–9
  changes with age 3, 6, 74–6,
    79–81
  see also the ear
hearing disorders
  noise induced 6, 15
  otosclerosis 6
  presbyacusis 6, 15, 35, 79–80
  recruitment 81
  tinnitus 6, 81
hearing loss
  amplification 83–5, 120
  and communication 75, 82–3,
    86
  and the family 87, 152
  assessment 76–9
  auditory training 86–7
  counselling 83–7 *passim*
    141–2
  management of 32, 39, 83–8
  psychological adjustment
    81–6 *passim*
  speech conservation 85–7
  speech discrimination 78–9
  speech reading 85–7, 120
hemispheric lateralisation
  15
home health services *see*
  community service
home help service, 99, 134
hospital-community barrier 106
hospital and residential care *see*
  institutional life, long term
  care
humour 11–12
Huntington's Chorea 56

iconic memory 7–8
insight 38, 57, 68
institutional life
  and communication 15, 100,
    114–15, 130, 157
  and communication
    disordered 31, 115–18
  and dementia 118
  and elderly people 95–7, 109,
    145

175

INDEX

and hearing impaired 87
and sociocultural factors 111
and speech therapy 31–2, 39,
117–18, 130
privacy 110, 113, 120–1,
124
residents attitudes 110,
112–14
roles 110, 115
rules of 109–110, 113
staff, 109–11, 113, 116, 139
intelligence 9
intelligibility 26
intervention *see* speech
therapy; families;
counselling
isolation 15, 29, 39, 101

Jakob-Creutzfeldt disease 56

Korsakoff's disease 53–4
Kuru 56

language
and aging 1, 4, 11–13
assessment 12–14, 22–3, 63,
69, 114
comprehension 1, 4, 11–12
expression 1, 4, 12–13
in dementia 63–4
language disorders *see* aphasia
language use *see* pragmatics
laryngectomy 28, 30
learning ability 9, 24–5, 32, 38
lighting 120
lip reading *see* speech reading
long term care 95–7, 99, 147
see also institutional life

management *see* speech therapy
memory
and aging 3, 7–9
and communication 11–12
and drugs 33
and learning ability 7, 9
echoic 7–8
episodic 7–8
haptic 7–8
iconic 7–8
in dementia 52, 57, 70
recall 7–8

semantic 7–8
short term memory 7
and speech therapy 31–2, 38
methodology *see* research
Motor Neurone Disease 49
multidisciplinary team
and dysphagia 28
and families 155
counselling 50–1
chiropody 99
family doctor 99, 106, 133,
137–9
general practitioner 99, 106,
133, 137–9
home help service 99, 134,
138
in hospital 132
nursing staff 46, 99, 131
occupational therapy 28, 99,
100
physiotherapy 27, 33, 99
psychiatry 46–7, 52, 54, 131
psychology 27, 46, 131
social services 46, 99
speech therapy and 19, 28,
135–40
structure of 130–3
volunteers 39, 99, 134–5
with dementia 67–9
with hearing impaired 77, 88
multi-infarct dementia 15, 54,
58, 66
multiple pathologies 3, 26–7, 31,
97

non-verbal communication 4,
14, 42–3, 82–7 *passim*, 93
nursing staff 46, 99, 131

occupational therapy 28, 97, 100
ocular diseases
cataract 5, 15, 35, 92
glaucoma 5, 15, 35, 91
macular disease 92
presbyopia 89
otosclerosis 6

Parkinson's disease
and communication 15, 17,
25

176

and dementia 56
and drug therapy 18, 33
and speech therapy 17–18
incidence 18
perception
 and aging 5–6
 and dementia 56, 61, 65, 70
phonology 58
physiological aging 2–5
physiotherapy 27, 33, 99
Pick's disease 53–4
pitch 14
pragmatics
 and aging 1, 13–15
 and dementia 52, 61
 and dysphasia 22
 management 100, 103–4
presbyacusis 6, 15, 35, 79–80
privacy 110, 113, 120–1, 124
problem solving 9
professional training 99, 130
prosody 14
psychiatry 46–7, 52, 54, 131
psychological adjustment
 group therapy 46–7
 to aging 47–9, 147–8
 to communication disorder
  24, 29–30, 36–47 *passim*,
  157
 to hearing impairment 81–6
  passim
 to institutional life 108–9
 to terminal illness 49–50
psychological testing 63–4
psychology 27, 46, 131
psychomotor abilities 6–7,
 13–15
psychosocial factors
 and aging 10–11, 101, 123–4
 and communication 14, 15,
  45
 coping behaviours 42, 46, 48,
  60
 life experience 32, 45
 roles 101, 104–5, 146
 sociocultural factors 10,
  32–4, 42

rate 13
reaction time 6–7, 33

reality orientation 71, 121,
 124–5
recall 7–8
recruitment 81
relocation 48, 108–9, 147
reminiscence 121, 123–4
research
 in dementia 71–2
 methodology and aging 4–5
 with families 148–9
residential care *see* long term
 care
residential care staff 109–115
 passim, 137, 139
respiratory system 5, 13–17
 passim
response rigidity 6, 8
reversible ischaemic
 neurological deficit 17
rheumatism 7
roles 36, 101, 109–10, 115,
 146–7

Schaie theory of cognition 7
secondary baby talk 111, 117
semantic memory 7–8
sensoriperceptual abilities 5–6,
 74–94, 107
short term memory 7–8
slowly progressive aphasia 67
smell 94
social identity 10–11
social services 46, 96–9, 106
social skills 86–7
somaesthesis 94
speech
 and aging 1, 4, 13
 articulation 13–14
 assessment 26
 pitch 14
 prosody 14
 rate 13
 see also dysarthria
speech conversation 85–7
speech discrimination 11, 78–9
speech reading 85–7, 120
speech therapy
 barriers to 37–9
 clinical variables in
  community 35–6

177

INDEX

cooperation of patient 32,
  38–44 *passim* 102–5
direct 18–40
economics of 104–5, 118
expectations of 31, 42
in hospital 99–101
in institutions 117–18
indirect 18–20, 39–40
intervention methods 36
materials 103, 104
patient variables 26, 31–5, 38
sociocultural factors 32, 34
with elderly 1–3, 9, 18–39
  passim, 95, 157
with visually impaired 93–4
see also aphasia, assessment,
  dementia, dysarthria,
  dysphagia, dysphonia,
  dyspraxia of speech,
  teaching
stereotypes *see* attitudes
stroke *see* cerebrovascular
  accident
subcortical dementia 54–6, 58
syntax *see* grammar

tardive dyskinesia 33
taste 94
teaching role of speech therapist
  evaluation of 139–40
  in institutions 115, 117–21

in multidisciplinary team
  130, 136–40
of general public 105–6, 157
planning 137
team *see* multidisciplinary team
terminal illness 49
tinnitus 6, 81
transient ischaemic attacks 17,
  54
transport 103–5

unconditional positive regard
  35, 43, 51

vision
  and aging 5–6, 88–90, 91–2
  and communication 15, 93,
    120
  and speech therapy 39, 93–4
  assessment 90–1
  cortical functions 90
  glare 90, 120
  psychosocial effect of
    impairment 92
  rehabilitation 93–4
vocabulary
  and aging 11–13
  and dementia 58–9
voice 1, 4, 13
volunteers 39, 99, 134–5